CORVETTE

THE RISE OF A SPORTS CAR

MARK EATON

AMBERLEY

To my wonderful, long-suffering and beautiful wife who has been there through all the ups and downs of life with me. Here's to many more years of driving beside you.

First published 2017

Amberley Publishing
The Hill, Stroud,
Gloucestershire, GL5 4EP

www.amberley-books.com

ISBN: 978 1 4456 6445 3 (print)
ISBN: 978 1 4456 6446 0 (ebook)

British Library Cataloguing in Publication Data.
A catalogue record for this book is available from the British Library.

Typeset in 10pt on 13pt Celeste.
Typesetting by Amberley Publishing.
Printed in the UK.

Contents

C2 Corvette Stingray logo.

Acknowledgements

My sincere thanks go to the following people for their unstinting help with this book:

Firstly to Jonny Bens, my friend from Belgium, whom I met through the Classic Corvette Club UK (CCCUK) and whose brilliant photography is the highlight of the book. That he gave so much time is very much appreciated. You can tell the ones I took!

Neal Stimpson, my dear friend of over fifty years, for his encouragement, proofreading, suggestions and general support. I couldn't have done it without you.

John Robinson, for supplying photographs and friendship.

Ross Thornhill, chairman and editor of the CCCUK magazine *Vette News*, for getting me into the whole thing in the first place, plus providing amusing anecdotes and support along the way.

Tom Falconer, Corvette author and expert extraordinaire, for his encouragement and insights.

The Committee and those members of the CCCUK who have encouraged, provided help and allowed their cars to be photographed and with whom I have had a good laugh over the years.

The owners of other cars that have been photographed – many thanks.

Any errors, although unintentional, are mine.

White 1988 35th Anniversary coupe.

Introduction

The Chevrolet Corvette has often been called 'America's sports car', but is this true and what constitutes such a vehicle anyway? There will, no doubt, be many opinions but most people would very likely say that a sports car is a smallish, two-seater car that is low to the ground, has little in the way of creature comforts and majors on performance. In terms of acceleration, top speed, handling and roadholding, it should excel or at least have a design focused on such things. It might also have a folding roof, the quintessential convertible. This accords with the Oxford English Dictionary, which defines a sports car as 'a low-built car designed for performance at high speeds, often having a roof that can be folded back'.

Quite a few might also say that the sports car should have its engine placed in front of the driver, although some would likely add that it might be better if it was placed just behind him or her. There will also be a very distinct group who will assert that it just must be at the back of the car – proving that, for some at least, more than half a century of effort constitutes a triumph of development over design.

What is true is that, for most people, the term appears to have some fixed attributes, while others seem to change with time and place.

To the author, the term 'sports car' usually conjures up, initially at least, images of two-seaters made by the likes of MG, Triumph, Austin Healey, Alfa Romeo and others. The very next images to follow include those indicating, shall we say, less-than-perfect manufacture and an alarming propensity to rust (coming as many did from a time when rustproofing didn't seem to enter the corporate mind of many UK and other European manufacturers). One might conclude that such cars only seem fast because they are low, uncomfortable and very noisy. This is not to say that such cars are not fun, charismatic and capable of engendering great loyalty in many owners, many of whom want them for those very reasons. Indeed, beautiful but relatively slow offerings from, for example, AC with its Ace and Sunbeam with its Alpine were completely transformed when the relatively small British engines were extracted and replaced with American V8s. Naming the new versions after dangerous and therefore exciting creatures was not just window dressing either, as the vast increase in power (or perhaps more relevantly, torque) pushed the older chassis designs much closer to (and sometimes over) their limits, even with upgrades. The same could be said for many a driver of such vehicles, but the Cobra, of course, became one of the great motoring legends and the Tiger has long been undervalued.

The concept of fun is central to the sports car – as is, for many people, a purity of purpose. In the past, this would be allied often with a simplicity of approach and execution, but these days, with legislation and customer expectations, this is probably no longer the case.

Some people really enjoy their cars; such enjoyment takes many forms and does not necessarily depend purely on cost or the latest fashion. A car should be fun to drive and own for the majority of the time at least (although some manufacturers major on this in their mainstream, non-sports car models). Many people will equate a sports car with speed. Speed in itself is not the evil some people would have you believe. Inappropriate speed is, however, very dangerous, whether due to conditions, circumstances, inexperience or all three. Speed gives many people a frisson of excitement, whatever is providing that speed. A car can still be a machine of the spirit (despite increasingly frustrating traffic volumes) and none more so than a sports car. Forget the job, the shopping, the chores, the errands, and all other mundane things – jump into your car and drive for the pure pleasure, freedom and fun of it. You don't have to break speed limits; just use those limits to the full, revel in acceleration, enjoy timing gear changes just right (or work with the automatic gearbox to the same effect), listen to the engine growl and sing, carve through corners, feel the forces and the fun, and then do it all again on the next stretch of road.

Automotive fun often equates to performance, either actual or perceived. Manufacturers are normally aware of this, although their involvement in such waxes and wanes. An example would be the advent of the 'hot hatch', when certain manufacturers took a family hatchback and fitted it with a more powerful engine, uprated the suspension, added initials such as 'GTI' to the name and thus catered for what became a relatively large segment of the market. They provided accessible performance and more fun than the normal models – at a price. These cars combined performance with the practicality of the base car and are still flourishing today. Indeed there are now versions from several manufacturers where the horsepower available exceeds 300 and the term 'hyper hatch' is being coined. In reality, the whole idea was not completely new, as there are other examples throughout the history of the car, one of which we shall be exploring in a little more detail later.

However good such cars were (and they varied), they were a compromise. A sports car offered much less of a compromise and, as such, had a smaller, more focused market. The sports car has never majored on practicality because it was never intended to. Most cars on the road are designed to seat four or more people and be able to carry their luggage, shopping, baby paraphernalia, bicycles and so on. Sports cars are, generally, unlikely to do any of those things and, if they do, certainly not as well. This is the entire point – there is no practical reason for such a car, with two seats, minimum luggage space, more power than necessary and nowhere to put the kids or the mother-in-law, while being low and difficult to get in and out of. Who on earth would hanker for such a thing? Quite a lot of people, it appears. Whether they all actually end up owning one is rather unlikely, certainly at the higher end of the market, but these cars are the ones whose images end up on the bedroom walls of young (and not-so-young) people. Dreams cost nothing, ambition can be a positive force and beauty takes many forms.

The automotive world contains a plethora of terminology, not all relating to technology. A 'sporting car' is not deemed, necessarily, to be a sports car, but rather one that has sporting pretensions, perhaps like the 'hot hatch'. The term 'supercar' has been attributed to the late, great and much-lamented motoring journalist L. J. K. Setright, although there is evidence that such a term was already in existence by 1920. The relatively recent term 'hypercar' seems to be a 'super supercar', apparently defined unofficially by extremes of everything – particularly price. Both of the latter terms can, however, be deemed sub-categories of the sports car.

Referring again to the Oxford English Dictionary, one finds a myriad of categories and sub-categories defining the word 'sport', but the first entries stand out:

I. Senses relating to play, pleasure, or entertainment.

a. Diversion, entertainment, fun.

It is interesting to note that, as early as 1919, one finds mention in *The Times* that 'The sports car, however, is not everybody's vehicle' (12 November 1919).

Enthusiasts have been making cars go faster since they first appeared, either by uprating existing vehicles or building their own from scratch (as opposed to using 'kits'). The latter is extremely difficult to do these days, such are the complexities, legalities and costs. So, fun, speed, acceleration, road holding and lack of compromise seem to be some of the hallmarks of a sports car as, no doubt, are good looks. Personal taste in all these areas is, as in all walks of life, paramount. The resulting affiliations and disagreements among owners and enthusiasts are fascinating.

So is the sports car 'in the eye of the beholder', so to speak? Very probably, yes.

Certainly it was in post-war America, where the inherent economic might and a wider world view had, arguably, come to the fore during the Second World War. This was accompanied by an air of exciting optimism as the 1950s beckoned. We all know that

Corvette owners like to drive their cars and getting out and about in a Corvette is one of the joys in life!

many American servicemen, who had come to the UK during the war, began affairs with English ladies named Em Gee (or the like) and they took their sweethearts home with them (or hankered for someone similar once there). Mainstream motor manufacturers were not really interested in this sort of carry on, but young customers were. So were enthusiasts within and outside of the industry. The rise of the Hot Rod went hand in hand with the rise of the sports car in the US. This quite clearly indicated that the younger customer was very much a group to be both reckoned with and sought after, as increasing freedom and plentiful jobs rocketed them into the 1950s. But, despite very small-scale offerings like the Muntz Jet (developed from the Kurtis Sports Car) and the Kaiser Darrin, Americans still had no sports car options on the mainstream manufacturers' showroom floors.

A different approach to motoring excitement would follow in what became known as 'muscle cars'. These were nearly always very exciting, but were basically production saloons (or sedans, if you will) with uprated parts. Some were outrageously uprated and extremely fast (at least in a straight line) and there was an assumption that cornering and stopping quickly was not high on your list of needs. Muscle cars, to which we shall return, form a separate, interesting and invigorating piece of motoring history.

The First Corvette

Meanwhile, at the giant General Motors (GM), a rising star named Harley Earl had set up what now would be known as a design studio or styling department but then was called the Art & Color Studio. Leaving aside the American spelling differences, he must have been among the first to realise the potential of styling and the effect such things could have on the emotions of potential buyers. The popularity of the British sports car (which offered swooping lines and raucous exhausts, and put fun over practicality) was not lost on him. He persuaded Ed Cole, general manager of the Chevrolet division, that GM could stem the rising tide of the Brits. Perhaps his greatest success was not in envisioning the car, immense though that was, but in persuading senior management to run with his idea in the first place! Ground-breaking thinking in large corporations (at least those outside of the computer-based technology industry) is rarer than they would have us believe. The fact that glass-reinforced plastic, or GRP, fantastically advanced as it was, was not only considered for the body, but actually progressed and eventually utilised, is little short of amazing. All this from Chevrolet, which was very much the 'bread and butter' division of GM, only used to delivering staid and steady products for the lower end of the market.

Ironically, it could be argued that it was a British man who went a long way towards solving the American sports car problem. The little-sung Maurice Olley was chief engineer of Rolls-Royce's American manufacturing division in Springfield, Massachusetts. After the Wall Street Crash enforced the closure of the British enterprise, Olley joined General Motors in 1930, where he worked for Cadillac for many years. He is credited with, among many other things, coining the term 'understeer' in relation to a car's roadholding. This is when the front of the car pushes wider while cornering than that intended by the angle of the steering wheels. In 1952, Cole asked him to head up research and development for Chevrolet; it was here that he found himself tasked with making Earl's vision of an American sports car and Cole's hopes for the same a reality. The former included creating a car with hitherto unheard of (in the States at least) levels of roadholding and handling. These were qualities, putting it politely, for which American cars were not renowned at that time. Such a challenge to a chassis engineer would merely be one of good schooling, sound thinking and a high degree of talent, but Earl wanted it quickly and the 'bean counters' wanted it cheaply, dictating that Olley would have to raid the GM parts bin wherever possible and make progress fast. These factors of speed and economy are all too real, but must have taken some of the spring out of Olley's step as he wended his way back to his drawing board. Our gallant Briton must have had talent to spare because, not only did he meet the requirements of his brief, but he exceeded them with some very neat work based on an 'X-frame' that put the new sports car (which became known as the Corvette) chassis ahead of anything else from American shores at that time and started a precedent that continues to this day.

Earl wanted the Corvette to debut at the 1953 General Motors 'Motorama' exhibition being held in January of that year at the Waldorf Astoria hotel in New York. This was an extremely high-profile marketing and promotional event that took place each year from 1949 to 1961, showcasing GM prowess with concept and prototype vehicles. It was intended to whet the public appetite for what a GM future might look like. Despite the very tight timescales, the new Corvette was duly unveiled to a very appreciative car-loving public. At last, America had its sports car! Or did it? The result looked good, being a convertible with sleek, modern lines. Rightly or wrongly, good looks are generally seen as important in life and this is particularly true of sports cars in most cases. But, underneath, the nascent Corvette was suffering from other problems. However, speaking at Motorama that year, no less a personage than the GM president himself, Harlow Curtice, sniffing the scent of sales, promised that the new Corvette would go into production in June of that year.

It is understandable that Chevrolet would not want to develop an engine specifically for what was a small-scale, specialist car and thus warming up the venerable Stovebolt Six or Blue Flame engine (as GM preferred), which was usually found in sedans, with a revised cam, increased compression ratio and triple Carter carbs was as good as could be hoped for. It must have been a happy coincidence that this engine displaced a similar amount (235 cubic inches/3.8 litres) as Jaguar's XK straight six in the XK120, which had been so admired by Harley Earl since its introduction in 1948 and had raised performance standards to new highs for a mass-produced car. It was this latest incarnation of the British sports car at which he surely wanted to aim the Corvette and not the smaller, much less powerful and hopelessly outdated MG TF, which was also launched in 1953. However, even 'hotted up', the old Chevrolet engine could only manage a very respectable but none-too-startling 150 bhp (brake horse power).

The real problems came with the transmission. It was not possible to solve a number of technical issues raised by the adoption of a manual gearbox in the time they had before the car had to be signed off for production, and so the decision was made to use the in-house Powerglide automatic gearbox. While this may have many good features in its own right, including being seen as very modern at the time, a two-speed automatic could not in any sense of the word be said to be in keeping with the sports car image of the time, and such a device could not be found on a competitor made in Britain.

Similarly, the Corvette was only available in white with a red interior – which is fine if you like that sort of thing, but not if you wanted any degree of individuality beyond your choice of car. Also, it had no wind-up windows and the windscreen leaked. These were things that a 'wind in the hair, flies-in-the teeth' enthusiast might put up with; however, the Corvette was expensive – very expensive – and the average American car buyer wanted more tangible quality. In the same vein, enthusiasts were not likely to be excited by the engine and were almost certainly completely put off by the gearbox. Seemingly to add insult to injury, it had a steering wheel from a Chevrolet sedan, ensuring that the owner never lost sight of its compromised and confused upbringing.

To be fair, the Corvette got along rather nicely for its day, but a manual XK120 in 1953 could (with decent fuel aboard) be purchased with 180 bhp or, if one paid for an example equipped with C-Type heads, 210 bhp. The Moss four-speed manual gearbox in the Jaguar may not have been the best of breed, but 'cog swapping' was still preferable, at the time, to a self-shifter for the enthusiast. It seems likely that the potential of the chassis was lost in the clamour over the driveline and thus did not make itself heard, which is ironic, given the engineering prowess it engendered. Also, of course, the Jaguar was no slouch in this department. Overall, in spirited driving, it seems unlikely that the Corvette driver would see which way the Jaguar went, let alone offer it any real competition.

It can thus be contended that Chevrolet bought about the ensuing dearth of sales themselves. A headlong rush was, apparently, thought preferable to sorting out the product's problems and producing more of what the market wanted. Earl had perspicaciously seen the potential, but this sports car did not seem to be a sports car after all. Getting publicity as a pre-cursor to selling was deemed all important, as seen by the Motorama rush. Unfortunately, publicity can work two ways: while they were no doubt very happy when the well-known entrepreneur and racing driver Briggs Cunningham bought a Corvette for himself, one wonders how the smiles at GM froze when, just one week later, Cunningham sold it, proclaiming it 'not much of a car'.

Perhaps Chevrolet was troubled by the imminent arrival of the Austin Healey 100, which had been unveiled at the London Motor Show in 1952 and would go on to be named International Motor Show Car of 1953 in New York. In unmodified form, this latest in a long line of British offerings set numerous endurance and speed records at Bonneville that same year. More powerful than the MG and less expensive than the Jaguar, it would become very popular in the States. However, taking the Corvette into battle against such opponents, under-armed and ill-prepared as it was, doesn't seem to have been the best way of going about things.

Many at GM saw the Corvette as more trouble than it was worth, and this was not the last time that this would happen in the car's history. However, despite the problems, there was enough enthusiasm high up to ensure it went ahead. The Americans may not have scored a home run at their first attempt but, to their credit, they went full tilt at the problem. It was all hands to the pump. One person drafted in was Zora Arkus-Duntov, another European émigré with talent aplenty, who had joined GM on the strength alone of seeing the Corvette at Motorama. The man, who wrote an impassioned letter to Cole and Olley in October 1953 in favour of the new car, would become famous for his strong, consistent and hands-on influence on the development of the Corvette. He found himself required to solve the rather alarming tendency of the '53 Corvette to allow its own exhaust fumes to curl back into the driving compartment while on the move. Here was another unfortunate trait unlikely to endear the car to potential owners. Whether Duntov's experience with gas flow was the reason for him being given this task is unknown (he had, *inter alia*, produced with his brother custom aftermarket aluminium overhead valve, hemispherical combustion chamber heads, using the name 'Ardun' for the by-then rudimentary Ford Flathead V8, which gained the car considerable power and him considerable reputation). What we do know is that the '54 did not suffer the same problem. From little acorns ...

One has to believe that Ed Cole knew that the new engine on which Chevrolet were working when the Corvette was green lit would work its way into that car, hopefully sooner rather than later. The Chevrolet Small Block V8 was pretty much everything the Blue Flame Six wasn't – light, compact, powerful and possessed of both more torque and development opportunity. Cole must have been pleased with the result, but we can be fairly certain that even he did not envisage it going on to be singularly the most successful internal combustion engine of all time, with production passing 100 million units by the end of 2011 and still going strong today.

The '55 'Vette (as it had affectionately become known) was transformed by its inclusion in 283 cubic inch (4.7 litre) form. Manual transmission was now available and a heady combination they made. Now the chassis could show off its abilities as the feisty little V8 pushed the fibreglass fantastic to hitherto unknown speeds and got it there much more quickly. Now success started to come the way of the 'Vette and this was built on year by year. 1956 saw the GRP body redesigned, with the 'rocket exhaust' tail lights and headlight grills being dropped in favour of a more aggressive front end and a smoother rear, with the adoption of the soon-to-be-famous coves along the sides. Colours other than white became available.

In 1957, the fuel-injected and most powerful version of the face-lifted car produced 1 horse power per cubic inch of capacity. While it was not the first to manage this, it was still a significant achievement in US terms at the time. This equated to a specific output of 61 brake horse power per litre, which was, indeed, very respectable; however it should be noted that, back in '53, the XK120 with the C-Type heads was producing almost exactly the same – helped, no doubt, by the breathing ability afforded by the double overhead cam configuration. A more effective way of comparing the performance of engines is brake mean effective pressure (BMEP). The pressure is theoretical and is a measure of how efficient an engine is at producing torque (and hence power) from a given displacement (or cubic capacity). Once again the Jaguar and the Chevrolet are neck and neck, with the former producing 154.1 psi and the Chevrolet 154.4. Compare these with the Blue Flame Six with 39 bhp/litre and 142.6 psi BMEP – you can see why the '53 was up against it. It also illustrates how the V8 was in a different league.

With regard to configuring their engines with overhead camshafts, it appears that Chevrolet preferred not to follow suit (with one notable exception, which happened much later and to which we will return), and has stuck avidly to the pushrod overhead valve (OHV) set-up for the Corvette to this day. They have steadfastly maintained that their engines produce the power required of them without the need of overhead camshafts (OHC), which is undoubtedly true. It is also true that, until perhaps very recently, increasing cubic capacity has always been seen as an effective and acceptable course of action if more power is required. Also, Corvette bonnet lines are very low, thanks to the cam sitting in the block and not on top of it, which helps its looks and gives leeway to designers in this respect. That the pushrod engine is considerably cheaper to make is not made so much of. However, in the author's opinion, the lack of OHC does not detract from the engines nor does the fact that they buck the trend. The whole idea of a 'lazy' or, at least, under-stressed engine is also quite attractive, certainly for a road car in which one wants to cover high mileages. However, it is probably one of the reasons that un-supercharged Chevrolet (and other similar American) engines are sometimes criticised for being inefficient by Europeans used to DOHC engines. It should not, however, be assumed that the Corvette was, or is, in any incarnation, slow or that some versions are not very highly tuned.

Contemporary press reports on the '54 six cylinder, the '55 V8 and the '57 fuel-injected version (both with manual transmissions) allow us to compare the performance of each version. The '54 got to 60 mph in 11 seconds dead and ran out of puff at 106 mph, having reached 100 mph in 40 seconds. The V8 dropped the 60 time to 8.7, the 100 time to 24.7 and went on to a 116 mph maximum speed. Quite an improvement!

The '57 moved things on again. The top-of-the-range fuel-injected (or 'Fuelie', as it became known) engine with a manual 'four on the floor' gearbox and a numerically high, mechanically low, final drive ratio of 4.11:1 could hit 60 mph in a scarcely believable 5.7 seconds and 100mph in 16.8 on the way to 132 mph. That car would be quick today, sixty years later! Perhaps even more amazing, for a 1950s production engine, was the way it revved. The low gearing meant that the car could pull 6,500 rpm in top, which was 300 rpm beyond the power peak, but it was possible to reach 60 mph in first gear (helping with the incredible time) if 6,600 rpm was used. At least one owner had regularly hit 7,000 rpm while racing a standard car with no apparent ill-effect! In such a guise, this production American V8 was anything but 'lazy'.

It is one of those imponderables as to whether it would have been better for the Corvette to have been kept under wraps for another couple of years. This might have allowed it to be launched with the new engine and gearbox, and for more of the other issues (including the poor fit of body panels) to have been discovered (and resolved) by GM, rather than by their customers. We will never know, even if we suspect, but there was one undoubted advantage of the Motorama launch, as has already been alluded to – the enthralment and ensnaring of one who would become known as 'the father of the Corvette'.

So was the Corvette now a sports car? It was certainly fast enough both in terms of straight-line performance and in the way in which it could be cornered. Comparing it to a competitor from the spiritual home of the sports car is interesting. The Jaguar XK120 had been developed through the XK140 to the XK150 by 1957. The usual received wisdom is that American cars are normally bigger than their European counterparts, but the Jaguar was 9 inches longer, 3.5 inches taller and 245 lbs heavier than the Corvette. Even in its most powerful version, the six cylinder's 210 hp and 215 lbs-ft of torque were no match for the fuel injected V8's 283 hp and 290 lbs-ft. The Corvette was some 6 inches wider but – given that it was already shorter, lower and lighter – being possessed of a wider track is usually what is called for in a sports car, is it not? Now it was the Jaguar that was likely to be left for dust.

Had something strange happened? Had the Brit become less of a sports car and more of a tourer? Had the American become less of a boulevard cruiser and more of a sporting car? A sports car perhaps?

It is worth reminding ourselves that car makers do not make cars purely so we can enjoy them. They make them so that they can produce a profit. By doing so, they can continue the process. In order to sell them, they have to design and make them so that we want to buy them, whether that car is to take us to the local shops and back and not much else; to travel long distances during the working week; to clamber up muddy slopes; to impress the neighbours; or to do any number of other things, including gaining enjoyment from them. Therefore, the challenge of the car maker is to work out what we, the paying public, want and try to provide it.

The American car industry appears to have made a rod for its own back, although they try to turn this to their advantage. I refer to what seems to apply to most, if not all,

American car manufacturers – the phenomenon of the 'Model Year'. In the UK, we are used to cars receiving a facelift around three to five years after introduction (although there is no set timetable) and then, if the model is successful (or times are hard for the manufacturer and a new model is not available), another one after a similar amount of time. Small changes could be introduced at any time, but are not usually made that much of. In the States, the car is designated by its model year, which, in the case of the Corvette, runs from the August of the previous year. New options are usually available, with possibly new trim and new colours rolled out to satisfy the 'new is best' attitude that American companies want to engender in order to encourage people to buy a new car every year, if possible. Every manufacturer has the same issue, so none of them can stop for fear of getting behind the times.

In 1958, Chevrolet apparently felt the public wanted their Corvette to be more eye-catching and so the car for that year was 2 inches wider and no less than 9 inches longer than its immediate predecessor. It also put on 200 lbs, all of which had to be accelerated (both linearly and laterally) and decelerated. Most noticeable was the new four-headlight arrangement, which gave considerably better illumination. However, the likeliest reason for their existence was that almost all of the GM cars were adopting them as a way to mark that year being the fiftieth anniversary of the founding of GM. There is a fascinating dichotomy in the styling, which depends on not only your point of view but also your point in time. Press reaction, generally, to the more highly chromed, ribbed bonneted '58 was that it was too fussy and detracted from the lines and business of being a sports car. At that time, the enthusiast might have agreed. Now, we tend to look on it nostalgically as part of the whole 1950s vibe, and '58s are much sought after. More importantly at the time, the buyers agreed with Earl and bought 9,168 Corvettes that year, which was 45 per cent more than the previous year and the best sales year yet.

In 1959, possibly stung by the press comment and needing, as always, to do something different, the car was somewhat cleaned up. The chrome spears were removed from the boot (or trunk) lid and the washboard bonnet or hood was replaced with a more conventional-looking item. Would the buyers be put off by this, given their enthusiasm for the '58? Well, no. They bought 9,670 Corvettes that year. To use an appropriate Americanism – go figure!

The introduction of a new, much cleaner-looking rear end in 1961 heralded the arrival of a brand-new Corvette two years later. In 1962, again no doubt anticipating the new car, the V8 engine was increased in capacity from 283 cubic inches (4.7 litres) to 327 cubic inches (5.4 litres). Despite the various visual changes and increasing number of options, there was a good deal of consistency under the skin of the first generation Corvette.

Before proceeding, it may be helpful to briefly explain Corvette nomenclature. During the design and development of what was to become the fifth generation of Corvette, the project was referred to internally as 'C5'. After its launch in 1997, this was adopted unofficially, but virtually universally, as a shorthand way of differentiating it from other generations. Of course, this then was applied retrospectively to the other generations and then progressed with later generations. At the time of writing (2016), the Corvette is in its seventh generation, known as the C7.

December 1958 saw Bill Mitchell become GM's head of styling. He was a total petrolhead, something that is not part of the job description for most car executives, but which perhaps readers of this book can appreciate, admire and applaud. Using GM resources that were not actually sanctioned, he (and those he directed) created a racing car using a chassis from the cancelled Chevrolet Super Sport (SS) racers, which were themselves styling and engineering development cars.

That is enthusiasm indeed. This 1959 GRP-bodied creation was called the Stingray and was very cleverly developed into the road car that became the C2 over the four years. Larry Shinoda was the man who wielded most of the pencils on both and, in the author's opinion, created one of the most beautiful road cars ever made. Another Mitchell-inspired concept car, the Mako Shark, was an additional element in the development, also showing many of the Stingray styling cues.

How it all began – the '54 was very similar to the first '53s, which all looked like this.

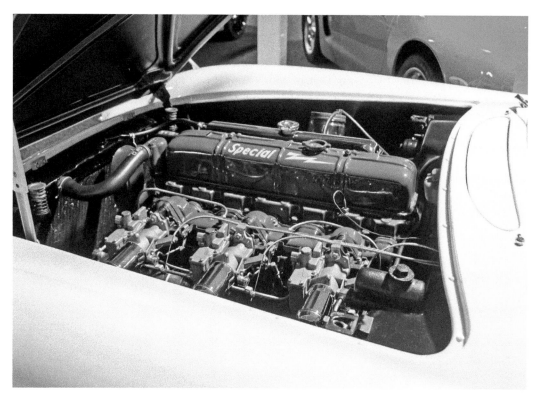

The six-cylinder Blue Flame engine in early Corvettes.

New styling, new engine – the 1957 Corvette.

A 1958 Corvette – note the four headlights and the chrome.

The delightful interior of the '58.

Above: For the last two years of production, the C1 rear end was redesigned and heralded the distinctive rear of the C2, which appeared in 1963. This is a 1961 C1.

Left: The motor car as art – 1954 C1 'rocket' tail light.

2

C2: The Stingray!

For the enthusiast, it is a good thing to be able to say that your car is based on a racing car (or that it has been successfully raced), so the '63 Stingray was off to a good start. It was also far and away the most sophisticated production chassis to be made in the US, incorporating, as it did, independent rear suspension (IRS). The C1, by contrast, had a solid or, as we say in the UK, live axle. Such a rear suspension arrangement has the virtue of being simple, cheap to make and straightforward to maintain. It also has the inherent advantage of ensuring that the wheels are perpendicular to the axle line. As with much to do with car suspension, carefully thought out geometry and accurate location of components is essential if one wants to get the best out of it. Bristol Cars were, for instance, acknowledged to be extremely good at this (and just about everything else too) and their cars had extremely high levels of roadholding and a good ride despite having a live axle.

One of the main drawbacks of the live axle, however, is that the whole thing constitutes 'unsprung weight'. It is easier (although not easy) to get a car to ride well if the amount of unsprung weight is low. This includes wheels and tyres, and is one of the main reasons for the adoption of wire, and then alloy, wheels (as well as better brake cooling, if designed well) – they are normally lighter than pressed steel, etc. You might not be very worried about a soft ride in your sports car, but you might be if the car is thrown off line by bad surfaces. If all roads were like race tracks, it would not be so much of an issue! Worse, of course, is that one wheel affects the other, as they are joined by the axle. Not only does this compromise potential roadholding, it also means that, when accelerating hard, particularly from a standstill, the torque of the engine tries to twist the axle around the centre line of the differential. This has the effect of making one wheel dig in and give good traction while the other is relieved of load and spins. The result, if you want to make rapid progress, is unseemly and unsatisfactory. It is possible to cure this by effectively tying the axle to the car, providing little, if any, suspension travel. This is how many pure drag cars are built and, while it works well with the extremes of power involved, it is hardly an ideal way of overcoming this shortcoming of the live axle in street use. Lastly, live axles sprung with longitudinal leaf springs (which they usually are) can also exhibit 'axle tramp' under really hard acceleration, particularly in powerful cars. This is even less desirable as it does nothing for either acceleration or the longevity of the car. Axle tramp is a violent, vertical motion caused by the winding-up effect of leaf springs by the torque being applied to the axle. The force causes the wheel to lift, the spring unwinds and the wheel drops, to relay the whole process very quickly. If you want to see what it looks like, get hold of a copy of the film *Bullitt* (if you don't already have one) and find the scene in what is still one of the very best car-chase sequences in cinema, when the now-famous green Ford Mustang of Steve McQueen, while in pursuit of what was in reality the faster Dodge Charger, overshoots a turning and has to reverse – in a hurry. Most people just see either the resulting 'burnout' or McQueen looking determined, but watch the driver's side rear wheel and the way it bangs up and down very quickly while the axle rotates. This effect is magnified here because of the very low reverse gear ratio (multiplying the torque further) and that the geometry is designed to reduce the tramping effect for a wheel rotating the other way, i.e. forwards.

Duntov was very keen on giving the new C2 Corvette fully independent rear suspension. He knew that, if well designed, it would allow the increasingly powerful Chevy to put that power down on the road and not just in a straight line. Power is not so useful if you spin it away while pulling out at junctions or out of corners. Roadholding can also be superior and our old enemy unsprung weight is much reduced too. Design is critical as, when wrongly designed for a given application, IRS can cause camber (the difference in distance between the top and bottom of the wheels on a given axle) and track (the distance between wheels on a given axle) changes in operation. This was demonstrated all too often on rear-engined vehicles designed in the 1950s (which, without IRS, would add the engine and gearboxes to the unsprung weight) and utilising the simplest form of IRS – the swing axle. Such an arrangement can (and often did) lead to a jacking-up effect, which *in extremis* results in the loaded wheel folding under the car and complete loss of grip and control of the car. The effect is exacerbated by the engine hanging out over the axle acting like a huge pendulum. This was the case with the Chevrolet Corvair, which became infamous after Ralph Nader's book *Unsafe at Any Speed.* Less appreciated is that the popular but highly flawed, original air-cooled VW Beetle ('Bug' in the States) and its dreadful cousin, the Camper, suffered from exactly the same type of geometry. The fact that they were so underpowered is possibly the reason that there were fewer issues than with the Corvair. Overall, IRS is generally superior to a live axle except in one important area – it is more expensive to manufacture.

Chevrolet was very aware and, indeed, seemed enamoured of the Jaguars of the day. Jaguar's famous IRS has, rightly, been held up as a marvellous design, utilising the drive shaft as the upper link and twin coil spring units for the lower arm. Not only is it very space efficient for an IRS design, the drive shaft is a fixed length; this means it can do away with the sliding splines required in other designs, which can be troublesome both in maintenance and in maintaining control of the car if the splines lock even briefly during hard acceleration. The only problems are ones of expense – in manufacture and in servicing. There are a lot of parts to make and put together or take apart. GM would never have gone for so complicated a design on these grounds alone. Duntov mimicked the drive shaft as upper link and brilliantly utilised a single-leaf spring for the lower arm on both sides. At least one famous journalist/broadcaster has made disparaging remarks about Corvettes having 'cart springs' *à la* live axles without understanding that the Corvette springs are part of an IRS layout and are mounted transversely, i.e. at 90 degrees to the car and to the way live axle leaf springs are mounted. Chevrolet knew a lot about leaf springs, as did all other American competitors – they never used anything else at that time and they were cheap. Duntov's arrangement had the added advantage of being very compact, taking up relatively little space. As part of the design process, the famously strong X-frame of the C1 was replaced by a ladder frame arrangement, which allowed a lower floor for the driving compartment and was then swept up to provide mounting points for the new IRS. Overall, it provided more room inside the car and, importantly, a lower driving position, which in turn would lower the car's centre of gravity – both are good for a sports car. It would also feel more sporting as the driver is closer to the road, which heightens the sense of speed.

Mention has been made of the beautiful body but it did have an Achilles' heel – aerodynamic lift. The clean front end is *sans* any type of chin spoiler and the air swoops down the curves from the transverse centre line and under the car without restriction. The curve acts like the wing of an aircraft. Such effects were typical of cars up to this and, indeed, later periods, but most cars weren't nearly as fast as the new Corvette. Perhaps this was really not too much of a problem for most owners, given the looks, handling, roadholding and acceleration of the Sting Ray – but, for racing, it really was noticeable.

As mentioned, the Sting Ray was launched in 1963 and, with the top-of-the-range, 360-hp, fuel-injected 327-ci engine and four-speed manual gearbox, it was capable of getting from a standstill to 60 mph in a little over 6 seconds and 100 mph in less than 16. It could also achieve a genuine 146 mph – astounding at a time when most British cars would struggle to crack 80 mph. The superb E-Type Jaguar had appeared in 1961, quite rightly taking the world by storm with its looks and performance. Contemporary reports have these two cars neck and neck to 60 mph and with almost identical top speeds, but the Sting Ray was quicker to 100 mph by over two seconds.

The C1 had only been available as a convertible. The 1963 Corvette Sting Ray too was available as such but, for the first time, offered closed motoring in the form of a coupe. This year was unique in that the coupe had a 'split' rear window. This was a victory for the stylists over the engineers and such cars are now much sought after. Not so attractive are the fake grills on the bonnet, again unique to this year. American cars have very often had a vast range of options available to buyers and the Corvette was no exception. In its first year of production, the new Sting Ray offered the purchaser a choice of four different engine outputs (from 250 hp to 360 hp), three types of transmission (three-speed manual, four-speed manual or two-speed automatic), seven external colours, four upholstery colours and twenty-two other options!

As had happened with the C1, and given the 'model year' approach, the Corvette evolved. Each year, there were numerous changes mainly in the form of improvements. Some are very obvious, but most are not. In 1964, the former was represented by the rear window becoming one piece and the fake grills disappearing. Less obvious was, for example, a three-speed fan being fitted to coupes to improve ventilation. Under the bonnet (or hood), the most powerful engine option now furnished 375 hp with the aid of fuel injection. For 1965, options (excluding the now six engine and four transmission variants) numbered twenty-eight. The two most significant features, however, were standard disc brakes and the option of a 'Big Block' engine. The former represented another significant move forward in developing the real world performance of the Corvette. Like many things in life, disc brakes were not a new invention at the time. Frederick Lanchester of Birmingham, England, an engineer of great renown, fitted a form of disc brakes to one of his cars as far back as 1902. The small American manufacturer, Crosley, also fitted a type of disc brakes to their Hotshot model in 1949 although, after a few months, problems saw them return to tried-and-tested drums. Disc brakes, as we know them, were developed by Dunlop and fitted to Jaguar's 1953 Le Mans entry D-Types and were considered one of the reasons why they took first, second and fourth places that year. Austin Healey fitted four wheel disc brakes to their limited-production, competition-based 100S in 1955 and, later that year, Citroen were the first to incorporate them in a true mass-production car in their revolutionary DS. Triumph's TR3 was the first volume sports car to adopt them in 1956. Meanwhile, across the Atlantic, Crosley's pioneering had been completely ignored, except for an optional hybrid disc/drum arrangement fitted to Chrysler Imperials from 1949 to 1953. Studebaker, a relatively small and advanced company, was the first US manufacturer to offer a true caliper style in 1963. Corvette had 'Heavy Duty' brakes and 'Metallic Brakes' as options since 1958, but they were based on drums all round. In 1963, a 'Power Brake' option utilising a vacuum servo was offered, but only 15 per cent of buyers went for this $43 dollar option. For unfathomable reasons, 316 buyers opted for drum brakes at a credit of $64.50 in 1965, discs being otherwise standard for the first time. Perhaps they were unsure about this new-fangled technology. This was unfounded as, although drums might offer good (even similar) retardation to discs initially (and Corvette drum brakes were very good of their type), as soon as the car's kinetic energy is converted to heat by the brakes, the drums start to expand. If this expansion passes a critical point, the shoes no longer have the necessary contact and, in short order, the brakes 'fade' and lose effectiveness. If not allowed to cool sufficiently, this fade can lead to total loss of braking. Discs are much more resistant to fade as there is no drum to expand and they are exposed to cooling air. It is an interesting fact that being able to consistently slow down a car effectively actually makes it faster. Late, hard and steadfast braking permits more time at higher speed, therefore allowing the car to achieve a higher average speed.

Offering a Big Block engine was fully in keeping with the times, as we shall discover. Chevrolet was like many manufacturers – it had to use its engines in a variety of vehicles and in various guises and states of tune. When the Small Block broke cover in 1955, Chevrolet already knew that, at that time, it was unlikely to be able to meet the needs of full-size cars and the ever-popular pick-up trucks, both of which would require more torque than the Small Block was likely to produce (again at the time). Work had already thus begun on a larger capacity engine known by the code 'W'. The first had a displacement of 348 cubic inches (5.7 litres), which was very close to what would become the most successful incarnation of the Small Block in later years, and rose to 409 ci (6.7 litres) in 1961 and 427 ci (7.0 litres) in 1962. These engines fall under the 'Mark I' banner. The 409 was the subject of a song by the Beach Boys in 1962 reflecting, within popular culture, a growing interest in both the speed and power of cars at that point in time. It is hard to imagine, these days, a popular artist including lyrics in a song along the lines of 'My four speed, dual quad, posi-traction 409', which refers to the number of gears, the fitment of two four-choke carburettors, a limited slip differential and the size of the engine in his car – more's the pity!

The Mark II was a pure racing engine of 427 ci that appeared in Chevrolet's record-breaking Impala NASCAR racer and completely out-classed the opposition at the

1963 Daytona 500. The Mark IV became the Second Generation Big Block (there seems to be no trace of any Mark III) and was a new design. In its first iteration, it displaced 396 ci (6.5 litres) and it was this engine that found its way into the '65 Corvette. Designed for much bigger cars, this 425 hp imbued the Corvette with performance even more electrifying than the fuel-injected Small Block. The option price of the latter was now over 65 per cent more than the former – an expensive way to have 50 hp less as far as the car-buying public were concerned. The fuel injection had also earned a reputation for being finicky and it was quietly dropped. Having said that, Tom Falconer, an Englishman recognised as a leading authority on the Corvette, states in his book *The Complete Corvette – A Model by Model Guide* that 'running right ... there are few American engines ... that can offer such a stunning reaction to a jab on the right pedal'. And for those that know how Corvettes pick up speed, that is some accolade.

Never had the now well-known adage of 'there ain't no substitute for cubic inches' been more apparent and the sophistry of fuel injection would not return to a Corvette until 1982.

The Big Block V8 displacement in the Corvette was increased to 427 ci (7 litres) in 1966 and became available with different carburettor configurations. This included the famous 'Tri-Power' set-up. Sold under Retail Production Order (RPO) L71 from 1967 to 1969, this arrangement had triple twin barrel down-draught Holley carburettors sat above the intake manifold between the two banks of cylinders. This was listed as the 427/435 option, where 427 is, of course, the displacement and 435 the quoted horsepower. So far, so good – but what is quite amazing is that only the centre carb was connected to the throttle pedal. So, in quiet (all relative with a Big Block) driving, only two barrels (or chokes, if you prefer an Imperial measure) were used. If one were to apply full throttle, both barrels on the connected centre carb would open wide, providing the engine with a large portion of petrol. This of course makes the engine pick up, and the intake manifold vacuum increases dramatically. The other two carbs are vacuum operated and this increase in manifold vacuum has the effect of opening the other four chokes fully! So, in very short order, one can go from having two part-open chokes to six fully open ones. One needs to have one's wits about one and preferably all four wheels pointing in the intended direction of travel, as the car will now being accelerating, shall we say, vigorously. Conceived in a period when performance was priceless and petrol/gasoline was less than 30 cents per gallon, it made sense, even if it was very much like pouring petrol into the engine by the bucketful! With an 11:1 compression ratio, it needed to be a high octane bucketful, too.

Small Block engines were available in 1966 and 1967 in 300-hp and 350-hp versions. The Corvette is a long-lived marque and, with the model year issues, was developed and improved year by year. As such, the '67 was deemed the best C2 year by many and is recognisable instantly by the reversing light above the number plate aperture. The C2 is now a highly sought-after model with prices climbing steadily, and yet it still represents the most amazing value in comparison with other classic cars.

The Sting Ray remains a beautiful car and a very fast one. Having independent suspension all round put it technically ahead of both Aston Martin and Ferrari at the time. The much-lauded 250GTO – which now change hands around the $50 million mark – did not have IRS.

The 1961 Mako Shark. One of the fully running design exercises in the development of the Sting Ray.

The 1963 Chevrolet Corvette Sting Ray in all its glory.

Above: Beauty and the Beast: sporting the famous split-window and side pipes – a dramatic if noisy option!

Right: Close-up of the one-year-only rear screen. This is the quite unusual colour of 'Saddle Tan'.

This is a '66 Big Block car, packing a 396-ci/6.5-litre engine under its curves.

The superb lines of a 1966 coupe. This car looks marvellous on aftermarket wheels and with this superb custom paint.

Last year for the C2 was the extremely purposeful 1967 model. This convertible has a 427-ci/7.0-litre Big Block power plant.

Inside a C2 convertible – a nice place to be!

A Chevrolet 327-ci/5.4-litre Small Block V8 in a C2. This is the base 250-hp model.

Another Small Block in a C2 but the fuel-injection system, clearly seen on top, helps give 375 hp in this car.

A C2 Big Block car with 427 ci/7.0 litres and 390 hp.

Curves, curves and more curves! The rear of a C2.

Surely one of the most evocative names in motoring!

A breathtaking photograph of a beautiful car – the C2.

3

C3: Stingray or Shark?

In 1968, the C3 was launched and went on to be the best-selling Corvette generation, partly due to it being in production for fifteen years. It was built not only on the progress the C2 made but also on virtually the same chassis. Again, it was developed from another Mitchell-decreed and Shinoda-drawn show car, the Mako Shark II (which in turn led to the 1969 Manta Ray concept car), and had dramatic front wings that sloped down towards the centre of the bonnet and a pinched 'Coke Bottle' waist. This made the car somewhat more snug inside than the C2. The whole effect was shark-like and thus earned the C3 its nickname. Under the skin, the same engine options were available as in 1967, with a 327-ci Small Block V8 (albeit a version unique to this year) in 300-hp or 350-hp versions and the 427-ci Big Block with 390-, 400- or 435-hp versions. There were also some special engines available – see Appendix 1: Muscle Cars and the Corvette. The Big Block provided drama, but the Small Block was the sweeter engine and put less weight at the front of the car, meaning it provided a sharper response to steering inputs.

In the transmission department, the old two-speed Powerglide automatic box was replaced by the three-speed Turbo Hydra-Matic 400, which had been available in other Chevrolet models since 1965. Somewhat bemusingly, the base manual transmission for both 1968 and 1969 remained a three-speed manual, with a four-speed being optional. Despite some initial quality problems with early cars, the 1968 car outsold the previous year by nearly 25 per cent, indicating that the new and striking shape had found favour with the car-buying public. Whereas the hidden headlights on the C2 rotated, those on the C3 popped up and, perhaps more interestingly, were powered (along with a flap at the base of the windscreen that hid the wipers) by engine-produced vacuum. Large vacuum actuators with relay controllers worked very well, although the perishing of the vacuum lines over time and inevitable leaks can be problematic later in the car's life. Many a Corvette of this era has appeared either to wink when one headlight refuses to raise or to look 'sleepy' if both can only partly rise! Renewing the vacuum system or replacing it with aftermarket electrics is often on the 'to do' list of C3 owners. The standard tyre for the car was of nylon bias-ply belted construction, which, if you are a stickler for authenticity, can still be obtained today. If, however, you prefer your tyres to provide more than the most modest level of roadholding, particularly in the wet, it is probably best to eschew these terrible things.

The '68 appeared purely as a Chevrolet Corvette, the Stingray from the C2 having been dropped. However, someone had a change of heart and the '69 received a single-word revision, becoming the Chevrolet Corvette Stingray. Both the single- and double-worded versions are surely among the most memorably named cars of all time.

The C1 had always been sold as a convertible. An 'Auxiliary Hardtop' had become optionally available in 1956, which could be bolted in place. In this configuration, the soft top could not be raised. This might be the preference in winter (in states where such an occurrence took place), with the hard top removed in summer. In the event of a summer shower (or worse) the soft top was then available. Some people opted for the entire deletion of the soft top (at no net cost), effectively making the car a hard top. The C2 offered the same convertible/hard top options but also a coupe as a full body-style alternative from the convertible; however, the latter had always outsold the former, sometimes by nearly two to one. The same was true of 1968, but in 1969 a reversal started, with the coupe being more popular than the convertible. Since that year, where a convertible has been offered, it has never outsold its coupe cousin. The reasons for this are, of course, not really known, but perceived safety was probably one, as many people suddenly became very afraid of a convertible turning over during a crash. On the other hand, it could just be about aerodynamics or distancing oneself from other drivers or that people didn't want to be so conspicuous – in which case, driving any Corvette was probably the wrong choice anyway! The convertible Corvette disappeared after 1975, not to reappear again until 1986 in the form of the C4.

For 1969, the stroke (the amount of vertical piston travel) of 327-ci Small Block was increased and it re-appeared as the 350 ci (5.7 litres). Small Block engines in Corvettes would remain at this displacement until 2005, when the C6 appeared. Buyers had the option of 300 or 350 horsepower. Big Block options remained the same as the previous year.

By 1970, the Big Block had been enlarged to a startling 454 ci (7.4 litres) but only had one version, with a quoted 390 hp and no less than 500 lbs-ft of torque. Interestingly, Small Block options started at 350 hp and ran up to 370 hp with the solid-lifter, high-revving LT1 version. There were two Big Block options in 1971, which also saw a one-year-only option: the LS6, which was quoted at 425 hp but probably produced more. This was the last of the really heavy-hitting Big Blocks. Many enthusiasts believe that the best years for the C3 were 1970–72, with the retention of the chrome bumpers of the '68/'69 at both ends, various detail improvements on the first two years and a good range of engines, unburdened by anti-smog equipment.

The horsepower figures quoted here so far are as quoted by manufacturers at the time. But times, they were a-changing. A lot of powerful cars (from all manufacturers) had been sold on the back of that power and the performance it imbued. Many owners were young and a good proportion probably had more money than driving prowess. Many accidents ensued and the insurance industry started, not surprisingly, to load premiums for performance vehicles. While there was inevitability about this, it was still good that such an era existed and many of the cars it produced have become legendary. There is a famous story that, while demonstrating the Cobra to prospective customers, Carroll Shelby would reputedly place a $100 bill at the base of the windscreen in front of the passenger. He would then say, 'If, at any time when the car is accelerating, you can reach that bill, it's yours.' Apparently, he always kept his money. It is this sort of allure that enthusiasts crave.

However, it is likely that the huge outputs quoted, which had helped in the sales war, were actually beginning to work against the manufacturers as cost of ownership increased or, in some cases, became prohibitive. While they had made no secret of it, the horsepower and torque figures quoted were gross. This effectively meant they were measured on an example on a test bed when the engine was not connected to any manner of ancillaries that it would be when mounted in the car. Power was not absorbed by radiator fans, dynamos, power steering pumps, etc. Also, the exhaust was extracted by a ventilation system and did not have to fight its way to the back of the car via tortuously routed pipes and mufflers. A much more equitable system is to quote output as net or installed, i.e. as the car actually is when you buy it. This was known as the SAE (for 'Society of American Engineers') net rating. Confusingly, at the same time in Britain, gross outputs were SAE and the net DIN! It is thus interesting to note that the 454 LS5 option was quoted at 365 hp in 1971 but 270 hp in 1972. Fortunately, the maximum torque produced was an honest 390lbs-ft at 3,600 rpm, which, for most conditions, would render a gearbox virtually unnecessary and, in real world driving, makes the car very quick!

So times were changing and just around the corner were such delights as the emissions issues and the fuel crisis. How would America's sports car fare? The less fun aspects of life were on the shoulder of the high compression, high lift cam engines of the 'muscle car' era and the Corvette was embroiled with all the others. Insurance and fuel costs are not subjects anyone really wants to dwell on – they are among the necessary evils in life, but they have their effect.

The C3 had had a strong showing in performance terms and, with its swooping wings and muscular stance, sales terms, too. Chevrolet, in positive fashion, set about adapting it for the new circumstances. Much seemed to be against cars in general and sports cars in particular. As is too often the case, cars were (and still are) seen by too much of the legislature as the root of all evil and, in this country at least, drivers are an easy target for taxation of one kind or another. I am all for protecting the planet, etc., but, if we had to rely only on public transport and bicycles, this country would grind to a halt in days. Cars can also give a measure of freedom to individuals that few machines can match, modern traffic volumes notwithstanding.

The early 1970s were also the era of the first version of 5 mph impact bumpers. In the quest to reduce injury, legislators and manufacturers often added insult – none more so, it seems, than in British exports to America. Who can forget what they did to the MGB, whose strongest suit had been its classic good looks, for which many forgave it its less than sparkling dynamic properties? The horrendous black bumpers, which were adopted for all markets and not just the USA, ruined its lines. We, in the UK, were spared what they did to American export Jaguars, however.

Chevrolet were much more imaginative and, for 1973, extended the length of the Corvette by just over 2 inches and adopted a body coloured nose made of a deformable urethane and, in 1974, a bumper of similar construction appeared at the rear made of two sections. This resulted in a one-year-only seam down the centre of this rear panel, which disappeared in 1975. The result was an integrated and natural-looking development that still met the Federal requirements.

Burdened as it was by low compressions and anti-smog gear, Corvette power outputs were not what they had been. People perusing facts and figures on the Corvette may be somewhat horrified to learn that, by 1975, the Corvette was only producing 165 hp in base L48 form, although 205 hp was available in the L82 version, and no Big Block was available after 1974. Early catalytic converters were probably not as efficient as they are today, but the main problem was that the exhausts from each manifold, instead of being of dual construction to the rear of the car as in previous years, were now routed into one pipe containing the converter and then branched out into two mufflers. This convoluted and crass constriction lost 30 hp on the L48 over the previous year and no less than 45 hp on the L82 – a reduction of 15 per cent and 18 per cent respectively. They also required unleaded fuel. I have heard non-Corvetters scoff that only the Americans could extract this little power from such a big engine. In cold fact, they have a point, but (and I shall keep returning to this) time must always be an important factor in car comparisons. The question is, what was everybody else doing? The reality was that the competitors were also having a hard time and, overall, it was fortunate that the Corvette wasn't cancelled altogether. It was kept afloat by people who wanted to recapture better days and have some fun in a grey time – something that says a great deal about the human spirit and the allure of cars such as the Corvette. Ironically, it appears that more than a few people traded in large sedans (which had to haul round large steel bodies with equally reduced power) for Corvettes because they could gain improved fuel consumption by doing so! If you had to sit at no more than 55 mph (the federally mandated speed limit from 1973 to 1987), a Corvette was much quicker than the sedan getting there and, once there, more economical and not to mention immeasurably more stylish! Overall, they still provided the sports car image and approach, albeit on a reduced scale.

While the power may not have been so impressive, people forget that, even in a low and anti-smog tuned state, the Corvette Small Block engine was producing 255 lbs-ft of torque in 1975, which is not an insignificant amount. In the UK, a Ford Capri 3.0 of the same era was producing 138 hp and 174 lbs-ft of torque, and was considered quite a quick and powerful car at the time.

1976 saw power upped slightly to 180 hp for the L48 and 210 hp for the L82; with the same specifications, 1977 became the best-selling year for Corvettes to this day. People still yearned for a fun vehicle, it seemed. In 1978, the twenty-fifth anniversary of the 'Vette saw a new swept-back rear window, replacing the flying buttressed 'sugar scoop', and both Silver Anniversary and Indianapolis 500 Pace Car replicas were made available. The C3 soldiered on, adding a new much more aerodynamic nose in 1980 (dropping the drag co-efficient Cd to 0.44 from 0.50 the previous year) along with a four-speed overdriven automatic with computer-controlled torque converter lock-up in 1982 for much more relaxed cruising. We were also introduced to throttle body fuel injection (TBI) in 1982, which helped to produce 200 hp and better fuel consumption and emissions, and rejoiced in the name of 'Crossfire Injection'. This somewhat Hollywood-esque nomenclature raised a few eyebrows (with one US magazine imagining a conversation including the phrase 'Watch out kid! That engine's about to crossfire!'), but it heralded the new fuel injection era and production Corvettes would not return to carburettors. However, it was now 1982 and the C3 could trace its lineage very closely back to 1963. It was time to move on.

This 1969 Manta Ray styling exercise was a slightly revised version of the 1965 Mako Shark II, which heralded the shark-like C3.

Compare and contrast the C2 and C3: a black 1967 coupe with its 1968 equivalent.

If you had seen this in your mirror in 1968, you would probably have moved over! The first year of the C3.

The muscular and aggressive 1969 Stingray. This concours coupe has a 427-ci/7.0-litre engine, tri-power carburettors and factory side pipes, giving 435 hp.

Still one of the most dramatic shapes on the road: a 1969 C3 convertible.

The flowing lines of a 1969 C3 coupe. With the T-Tops removed, the central roof spar can be seen.

Small number, big engine! This C3 bonnet badge indicates that a 7-litre V8 lurks underneath. In the background is a C6 Z06, which resurrected the 427 in 2006.

Seeing red – a 1970 Big Block convertible in Monza Red with red upholstery.

The interior of the 1970 Big Block car, with the driver and passenger looking out over swooping wings and a 454-ci/7.4-litre V8!

From the now sought-after 'Chrome Bumper' years – this is a '71 convertible.

Rhapsody in blue – a 1971 coupe.

The chrome bumper has gone, but the wonderfully integrated 'federal' version looks impressive and this 1973 coupe is very striking.

The author at the wheel of a beautiful '75 coupe with period-style aftermarket wheels. Behind the camera, the owner looks on nervously!

The last of the C3 convertibles – 1975. There would be no Corvette convertibles again until 1986.

1978 was the twenty-fifth anniversary year of the Corvette and the biggest change was a 'fastback'-style rear window replacing the previous 'sugar scoop'.

1978 also saw the Indy 500 race paced by a Corvette for the first time. This car commemorates it in bold style.

The changing, and much more aerodynamic, shape of the late C3. This is from 1982.

Last hurrah! After fifteen years, the '82 was the last year for the C3. This is a Collector's Edition model with glass hatchback – a one-year-only item.

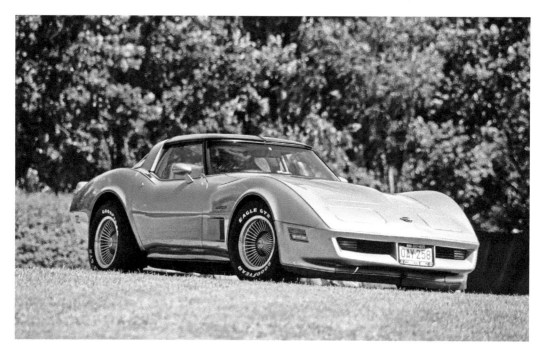

The '82 Collector's Edition again. Compare with the '68 and '69 cars; the overall shape is recognisable, albeit with many changes of detail.

An unusual study of a C3 showing the lights 'popped up'.

4

C4: Explosive Performance

There was no '83 model year Corvette, due to production problems, but 1984 saw the launch of a brand-new car, which became known as the C4. Still using the previous year's Small Block TBI V8, very slightly uprated from the 200-hp 1982 version to 205 hp, most everything else was new, including space age digital/graphic instruments (although these would revert to mostly analogue during a facelift in 1991). Corvette Chief Engineer Dave McLellan and his team had done a wonderful job. Stunning, modern looks – including a clam-shell bonnet/hood, which gave unprecedented access to the engine and front suspension (which now had forged aluminium wishbones) – were coupled to serious performance. The only styling cues from the previous model were the four taillights, the fastback rear window and pop-up headlights. The aerodynamics were vastly improved with a Cd of .34 and the new car was also 275 lbs lighter. Compared to the last of the C3s with the same engine, the slightly higher geared C4 took a nearly a second off the 0–60 mph time, completing the dash in 7 seconds dead, and over 1.5 seconds off the time to 100 mph (23.2 seconds). It was also 20 miles per hour faster at 144 mph, while fuel consumption was improved too.

McLellan knew that Corvettes had to handle and hold the road in line with current competition, and had gone to great lengths to give the new car these properties; it was likened to a track car. Certainly, on a track including the American's ubiquitous slalom course, the new car put in a very strong performance, particularly with the Z51 handling pack. In fact, one magazine found that, when comparing the latter to no less than a Ferrari 308 in terms of lateral acceleration, the much-vaunted and much more expensive Italian thoroughbred managed 0.8 g, while the home-grown upstart (which really should have known better than to turn up at all) put in a score of 0.95 g. The 308 with 255 hp and a manual box could reach 60 mph from a standstill in 6.8 seconds, a scant 0.2 sec quicker than the new Corvette. Although it would have pulled away from the Corvette from then on, the driver of the Italian car might have been more than a bit upset that his car was given such a close run for its money by the relatively inexpensive Corvette!

Unfortunately, the track car analogy was too accurate when it came to real roads, i.e. those that weren't track smooth – the '84 having what might politely be called a hard ride. The '85 was better in this respect and, once again, the car was developed year by year. There are some that believe that a well-sorted C4 can be the sportiest Corvette of all, not least because its relatively short wheelbase allows it to change direction quickly. This helps in the UK, where traffic roundabouts are prevalent.

The C4 era is unique in that it is the only generation that offered, for a while, a very special option – that of double overhead camshafts (DOHC) per bank. The endlessly fascinating story of the collaboration between the giant Chevrolet and the tiny Lotus is one that has filled many books.

While this book is about an American car with many excellent features, Britain also has a great history and reputation for engineering prowess, and can boast some of the greatest automotive minds across the years, not least now. That most of the Formula 1 teams are based here and that, for instance, the championship winning Mercedes engine was designed and built in Brixworth, Northamptonshire, rather reinforces this. However, we Brits have often been less successful at manufacturing, particularly in large numbers. Nevertheless, Chevrolet turned to Norfolk (England, not Virginia!) and the small but famous Lotus Cars to design DOHC heads for a very special version of its Small Block V8. As I have already pointed out, Chevrolet has generally fought shy of such complexities, but the decision was made to develop an engine that could power a version of the C4 to performance levels that would equal or exceed just about every other performance car made at that time, however exotic and expensive. They also followed another path to the same end by engaging Callaway Cars in Connecticut to design a forced induction system with great results, but in much lower production numbers.

An internal combustion engine is, effectively, an air pump, and combusts a carefully combined and proportioned mixture of air and, in our case, petrol vapour to produce rotary motion, heat and waste gases. While the design of an effective version of such a machine is very difficult to achieve, a fairly standard assumption is that, all other things being equal, the more fuel and air you can get into an engine and the faster that engine turns, the more power it will produce. Forced induction (supercharging) is one way to do this. More efficient, higher performance design is another. The Small Block Chevrolet (SBC) engines have two valves per cylinder, one for the inlet of air and petrol vapour, and one for the exhaust of waste gases. The bigger the valves relative to the combustion chamber volume, the more gas you can get in and out. But big valves are heavy (valves having to be raised and lowered in the cylinder head at high speed) and a spark plug has to be fitted in too, while ensuring the overall shape of the combustion chamber, including these things, is effective and efficient. Two small valves for each function can flow more gas than one big one.

As it turned out, the entire engine had to be re-designed and the development of what became known as the LT5 engine took around four years. In automotive corporate terms, this was good going. It was decided early on that the iron block of the standard V8 would have to go and it was replaced by an aluminium one. The DOHC 32 valve heads were also aluminium. In the end, only the displacement and V8 configuration were the same! The result was not only 375 hp (in the early version, with 405 hp in the later) but also excellent emissions combined with great smoothness and tractability. Its party trick was the ability to have a coin placed on edge on the top of the engine, which could then be started and run without the coin falling over. It is an extremely nice engine to drive behind: smooth, flexible, giving as good or better economy than its 245-hp iron-blocked brethren and as easy to drive in traffic. On the other hand, it has the instant ability to change nature and can rev savagely to 7,000 rpm and power the upgraded, manual-only ZR1 version of the C4 to 180 mph. With this, the roadholding and handling, the car that would become known as the 'King of the Hill' was born. This was a car that could mix it with the Ferraris and suchlike of the day, and at much less cost. With the cylinder heads, connecting rods and crankshaft made in the UK, it was also a good example of Anglo-American cooperation! The engines were assembled by Mercury Marine (famous for high-performance marine engines) in Stillwater, Oklahoma.

Was the sports car itself changing by now? Did people want more than just a good-looking two-seater with a good turn of speed? Some will always want the ultimate in performance and will put up with a lumpy idle, very noisy exhaust, unruly traffic manners and other issues in order to get it. To some, the whole performance world is an anathema and they are unlikely to be interested in any form of sports car. It appears that many performance two-seaters are now expected to be as happy going to the local supermarket as they are crossing an entire country in one go or out-accelerating everything in sight. If that's what the customer wants ...

The C4, especially in its later guises, seemed to meet this challenge head-on. Of course, money plays its part and the ZR1 was an expensive option, when the base LT1 (introduced in 1992) gave 300 hp without the complexities (and cost) of the small volume DOHC, returning as it did to an overhead valve (OHV) construction and, by 1996, the one-year-only LT4 (based on the LT1) was seeing 330 hp. Computer control of ignition and fuelling was enabling less exotic engines to push into territory not seen before, i.e. high performance with good traffic manners, good economy, etc. While these could have been added to the development of LT5 to move it ahead again, the costs were, rightly or wrongly, seen as too much of an obstacle.

Mention was made of the Callaway connection above, whereby GM sought to provide a limited edition, high performance C4 using forced induction. Callaway Cars of Old Lyme, Connecticut, were chosen as the partner for this venture. By ticking RPO option B2K on the order form via a select number of dealers, a customer activated a system whereby his or her C4 was diverted after production and shipped to Callaway, who would then fit a twin-turbocharged system. Turbocharging had been experimented with by GM prior to this, but Callaway had more experience in the field and, on reviewing the GM system, came up with their own version. A turbocharger is an exhaust-driven supercharger that forces air into the engine, thus providing more power. Deliveries of this option (which cost an extra 70 per cent of the base-car price) began in 1987, with power boosted from 240 hp to 345 hp and torque from 345 lbs-ft to 465 lbs-ft. Such numbers enabled this C4 to exceed 170 mph. In 1989, the price went up, but so did the power and torque – to 382 hp and 568 lbs-ft respectively. 1991 was the last year B2K was available and, by now, power had reached 403 hp and torque to 575 lb-ft. The car could now top 190 mph. Callaway could provide a number of options, including a full re-body to improve aerodynamics. One such car became a project for Callaway, known as Sledgehammer. After considerable upgrading in 1989, this fully road-legal car was independently timed at no less than 254.76 mph at the Transportation Research Center in Ohio.

However you look at it, the C4 seems to be one of the bargains of our times and can provide an awful lot of 'bang for your buck'.

The clean lines of an early C4 – 1986 coupe.

A 1987 convertible with its 1988 coupe cousin.

A really striking shape, this 1988 C4 convertible looks like it is moving fast even when stationary.

A 1991 C4 coupe showing off its nicely executed facelift.

King of the Hill – a 1991 C4 ZR1 with its all-aluminium Lotus-developed four overhead camshaft engine.

It's 1994, and this coupe shows that the C4 is still looking good.

A 1994 coupe with its 'targa' roof panel removed.

The final C4: this 330-hp 1996 Grand Sport demonstrates the C4 'clam shell' bonnet, which allows unprecedented access to the engine and front suspension.

A C4 Callaway with its aerodynamic body.

The same car from behind.

5

C5: Make or Break

The rate of change in cars was accelerating and, good as it was, the C4, after five years, was in need of replacement (despite which it actually soldiered on for another five years – see below). This was exacerbated by the fact that new side impact regulations were coming in for the '93 model year, which would require considerable expense to implement on the C4. So, the original plan was for the C5 to debut as a '93 car.

Towards the end of the 1980s, GM was arguably still the world's largest corporation, and in 1988 it posted a profit of $4.86 billion. Things looked good, but actually they weren't. Behind the scenes of this business behemoth, things were starting to go wrong – very wrong. By 1991, they had managed to turn a nearly $5 billion profit into a $2 billion loss in three years. GM was out of control. Many far-reaching decisions had been made over many years and it had taken a relatively long time to find out that many were wrong. Couple this to overly complex procedures and bureaucracy, and this organisation was heading towards the rocks with all the momentum of a supertanker. What it needed was a firm hand on the tiller before it was too late. Unfortunately, the 'captain' (Chairman Robert Stempel) was frozen with indecision, and his 'officers' were fighting among themselves for power, with egotism running rife and nothing constructive getting done. The sheer scale of the problems was revealed in 1992 when GM posted a loss of $24.2 billion – the largest in corporate history at that time. (It actually managed to exceed this in both 2007 and 2008, but that is another story.) GM was dying and the Corvette (after forty years of being their standard bearer) was dying with it.

The full story of how the Corvette survived these terrible times and was reborn as the fifth generation is a fascinating story of hard work, the very best of cerebral activity and pure passion, although it is beyond the scope of this book.

Enter then, the John Cafaro-designed C5 in 1997, a full four years later than originally envisaged.

Arguably the most important Corvette model ever, 'saving' the marque as it did, the C5 also introduced much-needed radical production processes in that the chassis rails were hydro-formed, i.e. by water pressure at 10,000 psi, had a completely new Small Block V8 known as Generation III (and termed LS1 in Chevrolet parlance), saw a rear-mounted trans-axle (including limited-slip differential) for the first time allowing 51:49 front-to-rear weight distribution, a drag co-efficient lower than virtually any production car at the time (Cd 0.29) and the best ride and roadholding compromise of any Corvette up to that time. The new LS1 provided 345 hp, 350 lbs-ft of torque and powered the car to a genuine 170 mph, but could give 30 mpg (although not at the same time). Note that this is the same power output as the first Callaway C4, which had virtually the same sized engine but without the need for turbocharging. It will sit quietly in traffic, not at all fazed by heat or red traffic lights, but when that light turns green it will sprint to 60 mph in less than 6 seconds. In 1999, the C5 had the option of a 'Head-Up Display', whereby key information for the driver (road speed, engine revs and the information from one other dashboard instrument plus warning lights) is projected onto the windscreen directly in front of the driver. This means that, while driving, the driver of a C5 so equipped does not need to take his or her eyes off the road in order to read the instruments. The idea comes from fighter planes and was introduced by Chevrolet on the C5 many years before BMW produced a similar system. Dual-zone climate control was one of multiple options that could turn your fifth-generation Corvette into a very comfortable car if, indeed, you should so desire.

The C5 has, like all the late-model cars, a Jekyll and Hyde character too, in that it can cruise long distances quite quietly and economically, with the aforementioned dual-zone air conditioning keeping the temperature in the driving compartment cool and comfortable and the sound system playing your favourite tunes, or it can take you to the local shops in heavy traffic and not miss a beat. On the way back, one can take a dual carriageway or the back roads and it can really show its performance side, all with a marvellous V8 soundtrack. This will be a burble at slow speed and low revs, with a lovely growl as one opens it up building to a NASCAR-style hammering thunder approaching the red line.

A willingness by the Corvette engineers to find innovative solutions to the problems raised in car design and manufacture can be nicely illustrated by the fact that, with a very ambitious weight target for the new car (which, of course, helps all aspects of performance including fuel economy), balsa wood was used as the filling for a composite sandwich in the floor panels, having been found to have the best characteristics of strength, weight and sound deadening.

The engine is the heart of the car and the sounds made by V8s, especially American ones, are utterly addictive. As an engine, the Small Block Chevrolet (SBC) is up with the best of them, something proved by the fact that it has been produced in greater numbers than any other internal combustion engine – ever. This Corvette had the latest incarnation – a completely new design that continued the tradition of a 90-degree V8 with push rod actuation of the valve gear and displaced 346 ci or 5.7 litres. This was a clean sheet design, though, bringing the latest technology to the tradition. The Americans have always been excellent at thin wall casting – one of many reasons for the success of their engines. Now the GM people turned their skills from casting iron to casting aluminium. Various Corvettes have had aluminium cylinder heads and the C4 ZR1 had an aluminium block too. However, the new LS1 was the first to have both in the base engine.

Taking a quick look at the features from the top of the engine down, we find that, under the rather nicely executed cosmetic covers, there are eight coil packs, which individually fire the sparking plugs in conjunction with the electronic ignition system. The fuel-injection system is sequential and the throttle is 'fly-by-wire' electronic, i.e. there is no physical throttle cable. The inlet manifold is a one-piece composite item with tuned length runners. While this type of material is now commonplace, at the time it was a relatively new idea. Compared to metal manifolds, it reduces heat soak from the engine, allowing the intake air to be cooler, thus increasing power for a given ambient temperature. It is also lighter. The heads were the most free-flowing base engine heads yet, with 'cathedral' porting. 2.02-inch inlet and 1.55-inch exhaust valves (one each per cylinder) are raised by hydraulic roller lifters and returned to their seats by 'beehive' springs. The camshaft is machined from billet steel and is rifle drilled to save weight. The exhaust manifolds do not look particularly interesting, but are, in fact, hydro-formed from stainless steel and double skinned. This has the effect of not only reducing under-bonnet temperatures but also of allowing exhaust temperatures to rise quickly from start-up to ensure fast catalytic converter 'light-off', which, unsurprisingly, helps with emissions.

Pistons are cast aluminium solid-skirt slipper type by Mahle of Germany, with a compression ratio of 10.0:1. The firing order was changed from the traditional SBC 1-8-4-3-6-5-7-2 to 1-8-7-2-6-5-4-3 to help eradicate the possibility of the mixture leaning out between cylinders 5 and 7, and to reduce vibration and increase idling smoothness. It also accounts for the different exhaust sound at idle from the SBC. The connecting rods are forged, sintered steel that have been shot peened, while the crankshaft is cast from nodular iron and is also rifle drilled with undercut and rolled fillet journals. While some might, as usual, snipe at the 'simplicity' of an OHV design, this is a magnificent engine that spawned a whole range of 'LS' versions, which have found their way into many vehicles from pick-up trucks to transplants in some TVRs, perhaps the most individual of English sports cars. From 2001, the LS1 was producing 350 hp and up to 375 lbs-ft of torque.

To compare cars and highlight thirty years of development, a mainstream American magazine ran an article comparing the then new '97 (with its 346-ci/5.7-litre engine) to a '67 with a 427-ci Big Block. In all performance comparisons, the newer car was, bluntly, in a different league, despite having an engine 20 per cent smaller in capacity. It accelerated quicker, braked quicker, went much faster and held the road much more tenaciously, while using half the fuel. It also had much more room and equipment, including safety-related items. Nobody should be surprised or disappointed by this. In measurable terms, thirty years of work should show improvement! However, the authors summed it up very elegantly by saying that, despite the figures, 1967 was still a very nice place to be! The whole fun and enjoyment issue again – which is not measurable, but we, the enthusiasts, know the difference.

Meanwhile, in typical Corvette fashion, the C5 was developed each year. It was available in three body shapes: coupe, convertible (from 1998 on) and, for the years 1999 and 2000, as a manual-only 'Fixed Roof Coupe', which had a boot (or trunk) rather than the hatchback compartment of the coupe. The fixed roof connation indicates, correctly, that the coupe did not have a fixed roof. All coupes had a removable panel, which covered the area from the top of the windscreen and the top of the B-pillar, i.e. the area over the driver and passenger. One could have this panel as either a solid, body-coloured version (as standard) or as a very dark blue transparent one – or indeed both, if one desired. The transparent top looks virtually black from the outside, making a nice contrast to the bodywork, particularly with cars painted in light hues. Although heavily tinted, it lightens the interior considerably. The C3 began the Corvette tradition of removable roof panels (hence making a roofless or 'targa'-style car) with two on a T-shaped frame, which results in the name, unsurprisingly, of 'T-Top'. The C4 moved to a single panel, but this was probably a marketing afterthought, as removing it rather weakened the structure, which was already more flexible than it could have been. In an attempt to counter this unwelcome move from a chassis point of view, engineers insisted that the roof be bolted in place, which restores some of the rigidity. Removing the roof panel from a C4 coupe requires a spanner, ideally two people, some time and not a little patience. The C5 combined the best of both of its forebears with a single-piece roof, *à la* the C4, but with three simple catches that make removal a one-person job of but a few seconds. It also allowed for rather neat stowage in the luggage compartment, with specifically engineered mounting and locking points, albeit at the expense of some luggage room.

The C5, like all Corvettes, was quite quick for its time but the short-lived Fixed Roof Coupe became the Z06 (borrowing the nomenclature from a 1963 limited road-going race option) in 2001 with increases in power to 385 hp and then 405 hp in 2002. This was the 'high performance' version of the C5, available only with manual transmission and featuring upgraded suspension and various lightened components, including an exhaust system made from titanium, a first for a mass-produced vehicle. This saved 19 lbs over the steel version and, together with thinner glass in 2002 that saved 2.2lbs, showed the commitment the Corvette team had to further weight saving and, therefore, performance. The Z06 had larger front anti-roll bars (or sway bars in US parlance) and re-valved rear dampers. It appears from most press commentary that, whatever these changes actually were, at the time they made a considerable difference. The author has long contended that the damper and/or spring rates on C5s do not seem to suit British (i.e. bumpy) roads and the comments from the motoring press tend to back this up. In order to make the above-mentioned increases in power, the LS1 received a new camshaft, higher flow inlet and exhaust manifolds, revised cylinder heads, higher flow rate fuel injectors and a 6,500-rpm red line (up from 6,000), becoming the LS6 in the process.

The Corvette story nearly ended after the C4 and it was, at times, touch and go as to whether the C5 would ever see the light of day as a production car. We have some very brave, ingenious and cunning people to thank for this. This Corvette was developed by sometimes breaking the rules, but in clever if not downright devious ways! This showed a passion for the vehicle and its history by the engineers and other members of the Corvette team at GM far beyond what might expect for an (animate) inanimate object!

The author's 1999 C5 coupe happily adapts to carrying his daughter to her wedding.

The clever curves and resultant superior aerodynamics are clearly evident in the author's '99 coupe. The strake running along the door is a factory extra.

The Chevrolet Generation 3 LS1 Small Block V8.

The Corvette has paced the Indy 500 thirteen times – more than any other marque. This is the particularly vivid 1998 version.

This 2001 C5 coupe in profile shows the smooth, stunning lines of John Cafaro's design.

The C5 was designed as a convertible from the outset. This is a 2003 example.

The C5 coupe was one of the most aerodynamic cars of its era. This is a beautiful example of a fiftieth anniversary commemorative car from 2003.

The C5 Z06. This astounding 2003 example has received some subtle upgrades, is a show winner and looks ready for take-off!

C5s of various vintages at the Classic Corvette Club UK's National Show.

Corvettes have been modified by some owners since the marque began. This C5 convertible is quite an extreme example with wide body panels.

Whether in light shades or dark such as this, the C5 retains its allure.

Clearly displaying its hard top styling, the front splitter and tail spoiler are nicely integrated extras on the C5 Z06.

6

C6: The Power Keeps on Coming!

It is approaching the 2005 model year, and Corvette fans around the world eagerly await the unveiling of the new C6. The usual rumours about a mid-engined Corvette had done the rounds but GM was in no position financially to make such radical changes. Thus the familiar front engine layout was revealed. As usual, opinion was divided on the looks, not least because, for the first time since the C1, the headlights were fixed and this generation was probably closer in looks to the previous one than any other.

The C6 launched with the most powerful base engine ever offered – the 400-hp Gen IV LS2. Again, this was a development of the LS1 and displaced 6.0 litres/366 ci. Despite this, in the C6, it provided better fuel economy. The body was 5 inches shorter and 1 inch narrower than the C5, although the wheelbase was 1.2 inches longer. The Cd (co-efficient of drag) reduced slightly to 0.286 and, remarkably, the car was lighter than the C5 by 67 lbs. Remarkable because, if one cares to take a look at each new version of an existing car, these days it tends to be heavier than its forebear. No doubt this is because of increased safety strengthening and the plethora of equipment now expected. A small increase in kerb weight is seen as a good result, so a reduction is extremely good. The LS2 produced 400 lbs-ft of torque, which would have pushed the safe capacity of the 4L60-E automatic transmission found in the C5, so the improved and sturdier 4L65-E was adopted.

As would be hoped, the development moved the C6 on from the C5 in just about every way, albeit only marginally in some areas. GM claimed performance figures of 0–60 mph in 4.1 seconds and a top speed of 186 mph. In reality, of course, very few people are going to max out a Corvette on public roads, excluding, perhaps, those lucky enough to be able to use the dwindling number of unrestricted autobahns in Germany. It is of interest mainly in terms of conversation or even for your own quiet knowledge. Similarly, in order to extract the fastest possible acceleration times, professional testers have to be brutal with the car, certainly if it is equipped with manual transmission. The technique is to judge the optimum amount of revs (to avoid the car either bogging down or excessively spinning its wheels), set these with the right foot and, having engaged first gear, sidestep the clutch. Thus the clutch engages purely on the strength of the springs, with no tempering from the driver, i.e., it goes from fully disengaged to fully engaged in the time it takes the pedal to get from the floor to its normal resting place. Also one has to use trial and error to find the aforementioned optimum number of revs, and so this violent treatment of the driveline happens many times, something a careful owner would normally avoid. Launch control is becoming more common on high-end performance cars (including Corvette), but again must put a lot of strain on the driveline of the vehicle.

The LS2 only lasted three years before being superseded by the 6.2-litre/378-ci LS3, which gave 432 hp and 424 lb-ft of torque in 2008 – yet another excellent LS engine and yet another highest base engine output.

In 2006, the Z06 moniker was reintroduced for the carbon-composite winged, aluminium-chassised 7-litre version of the C6. 3 inches wider than the base car but, with a chassis 30 per cent lighter, the 427 was back and how! Although somewhat bemusingly still designated a Small Block, this hand-assembled gem could rev to over 7,000 rpm and produced a genuine 505 hp. It was the first engine to hold the new Certified SAE rating, which guaranteed the stated output. Available with manual transmission only and with uprated suspension, this car, which is quite capable of spinning its wheels at 100 mph in the dry, was the fastest ever production Corvette at the time.

It held that honour for only two years, when Chevrolet introduced a supercharged version of the LS3 (called LS9) in the ZR1 – a term used to designate the high-performance version of the 1970–72 C3s. This modest configuration, sporting an Eaton twin rotor/ four lobe, Roots-type positive displacement supercharger between the banks of cylinders, produced 638 hp and 604 lb-ft of torque, and was the most powerful production engine ever offered by General Motors. Capable of just over 200 mph, with 60 mph coming up in less than 4 seconds and 100 in less than 9, the ZR1 could mix it with the very best of supercars, such as the Lamborghini Murcielago 670SV, which cost nearly three times as much. To hammer this home, the ZR1 had a special version of the Magnetic Selective Ride (MSR) system, first introduced on the 2003 version of the C5. Many cars, including Corvette, had a selective system whereby the flow of fluid in the dampers (often erroneously called shock absorbers) is regulated by mechanically restricting orifices. The MSR used a synthetic magneto-rheological fluid, which held particles of iron. Varying electrical current through this fluid caused the iron particles to align so that they restricted the flow. This produced a much faster response from the dampers. In fact, it could alter the flow rate, and hence the amount of damping, at up to 1,000 times a second. This equates to being able to alter the ride for each inch of road at 60 mph!

Transmission wise, only a (strengthened) manual gearbox was offered and, to help cope with the torque, the normal single-plate clutch was replaced by a twin-plate item. GM turned to the renowned Italian brake maker, Brembo, for the brakes to stop this road rocket and they went the whole hog, specifying as standard (not optional as with most exotic manufacturers) carbon-ceramic discs, which were a massive 15.5 inches in diameter at the front and 15 inches at the rear. Calipers were six-piston at the front and four at the back. This is racing car technology, and it produced astounding braking ability on the road. Also from racing came the use of carbon fibre components to reduce weight, which had been seen in various parts in the Z06 version; however, the ZR1 bonnet/hood (with a rather debateable clear polycarbonate window in it showing the supercharger cover), the fixed roof panel, roof bow, rocker panels (or sills) and front splitter were all made from it.

Perhaps in order to encourage sales, the Grand Sport name also returned in 2010. This combined many features of the Z06, including, most obviously, the wider body, with some specific ones (e.g., a slightly revised nose) but retained the LS3 engine and transmission. The intention, presumably, was to major on higher levels of roadholding, which is fine and was no doubt achieved; however, one can't help recalling that the original 1963 Grand Sport had one of the most fearsome engines ever fitted to a Corvette and that this moniker might have been better applied to the ZR1. The C6 Grand Sport is, however, a very striking car.

2013 saw the last year for production of the C6 range and, as ever, technology, requirements and expectations had moved on. The Corvette had to, too.

2005 – the first year for the C6.

The clever lighting of this shot of a 2006 coupe shows off the detail of the evolutionary C6 lines.

Move over! A 2005 Z06 in its rightful place – the outside lane!

Elegant aggression – a C6 Z06 dominates the street.

A 2007 C6 convertible in a green and pleasant land.

The left-hand drive is surprisingly easy to manage in the UK and makes foreign trips easy! This 2007 has automatic transmission with 'paddle-shift'.

This elevated shot of a Z06 clearly shows the smooth lines around the passenger compartment and the 'lip spoiler' on the tail, both of which help the aerodynamics.

Now sporting a 6.2 LS3 V8 with 430 hp, a 2008 C6 coupe looking purposeful.

The Corvette passes the 600-hp mark. This is a 638-hp 2012 ZR1 Centennial Edition looking menacing.

The astoundingly fast ZR1 needed astounding brakes! Here are the Brembo six-piston front calipers with 15.5-inch carbon-fibre-reinforced ceramic silicon carbide discs.

A 2013 C6 Grand Sport convertible – this particular car was the only one made to the specification shown.

Another striking Indianapolis Pace Car – this is the C6 from 2008; the second time a C6 was honoured thus.

Although steely in demeanour and colour, this C6 Grand Sport is, as Corvettes have always been, bodied in GRP.

2007 C6 Pace Car convertible, seen in front of a Spitfire.

7

C7: Return of the Stingray

The 2014 model year produced the C7, on which the Stingray name was resurrected and conferred; the car that wears it is being proclaimed by all as probably the best Corvette yet, and a significant step forward from the C6. Another new Small Block V8 engine was created, again with 6.2 litres and with another previously seen reference of LT1, producing 455 hp and 460 lb-ft of torque (or 460 and 465 respectively with the Z51 Performance Package, which included a switchable exhaust, i.e. from relatively quiet to high flow and noisy). Yet another new base engine power record! L. J. K. Setright was of the opinion that a car whose engine produced very similar figures for power and torque was usually nice to drive in the real world, and Corvettes have often had this advantage. For a road car, if similar figures are not available, then more torque than power is normally preferable to the opposite, and again there are Corvettes that provide this. This LT1 also introduces 'displacement on demand' (or 'Active Fuel Management', as Chevy calls it), allowing four of the eight cylinders to be automatically shut down when cruising on a light throttle to save fuel. Full displacement is returned when the throttle opening demands it. Other firsts for the Corvette include continuously variable valve timing and direct fuel injection, which, through extremely high pressure, allows more accurate and complete combustion.

Once again, the new body shape caused some controversy, though overall it is very striking and in keeping with the high visual impact for which Corvettes have always been known. The Cd of 0.29 includes an element of true downforce, another first for Corvette. This means the aerodynamics over, under, around and through the car are even more efficient than previous models with a similar co-efficient as downforce, by its nature, creates drag. During tests, the car, fitted with a manual gearbox, recorded a 0–60mph time of 4.4 seconds and reached 100 from a standstill in 9.4 seconds. The car will exceed 180 mph and, with the manual gearbox will achieve this in fifth, sixth and seventh! This shows the consideration given to economy, where 'tall' gearing means lower revs and the use of less fuel. The latter gear provides no less than 48.4 mph/1,000 rpm. The car has seen 1.15 g lateral acceleration through corners, comfortably exceeding the officially stated 1.03 g. But this initial iteration of the C7 will go down in history as the first Corvette to get almost all positive comment on the BBC's *Top Gear* programme. It firmly cemented the stated subjective opinion by lapping their Dunsfold circuit in 1 minute 19.8 seconds, which is the same as a Ferrari 599 and only 0.6 seconds slower than the highly respected, mid-engined Ferrari 458 Italia that costs about three times as much. And this (albeit with Z51) is the base model!

As if to underline the latter point, Chevrolet introduced the Z06 version for 2015 with a supercharged LT1 named LT4 (both engines mimicking the latter years of the C4). Power and torque have the same number – an incredible 650 – both exceeding the C6 ZR1 and thus taking the crown for the most powerful GM engine to date. It keeps the Active Fuel Management and variable valve timing of the LT1, and adds some sophistry of its own in having titanium intake valves and connecting rods.

This immediately raises the question of whether there will be 'ZR'1 version, whether it be called that or not or whether a mid-engined Corvette is waiting somewhere in the wings. Such rumours are always doing the rounds, although this time there may be more to it.

There are two aspects that might be called unusual in that neither were available on the previous models; the options of both convertible and automatic versions. The latter is a true automatic and not a twin-clutch or similar arrangement. No version of the latter could be found that could handle torque, packaging and weight requirements. So Chevy built its own, which weighs only 8 lbs more than the manual. It has no less than eight ratios, and a car so equipped is faster than a manual apparently, with Chevy claiming 2.95 seconds to 60 mph. The manual version has another industry first in 'Active Rev Matching', which, as the name suggests, has the car 'blip' the throttle to ensure perfect synchronisation on down changes. For those that want to attempt this fun function themselves, the system can be switched off.

The latest generation and the revival of a famous name – a 2014 C7 Stingray coupe.

The Stingray has a drag co-efficient of 0.29 as per the C5 and C6, but has an element of downforce not included with its forebears.

The most powerful production Corvette yet, the 2015 C7 Z06 packs no less than 650 supercharged horsepower.

LT4 – the powerhouse of the C7 Z06. The Eaton supercharger is situated beneath the fluted cover between the banks of cylinders and helps create 650lbs-ft of torque.

This shot of another 2015 C7 Z06 clearly shows the wider body and arches compared to the Stingray.

No generation has had a convertible version of its most powerfully engined model – until now, with the 2015 Z06 convertible.

The C7 has LCD instruments that can be switched between various configurations. This car has the eight-speed paddle-shift automatic gearbox.

This C7 Z06 looks both civilised and stylish. One moment it is – the next, it is one of the fastest road cars in the world.

It may be a 200 mph car, but the C7 Z06 is quite at home in the city when required.

Conclusion

The question originally asked was: is the Corvette a sports car? This led to examining what a sports car is and how this concept developed. The Corvette developed, too. Were they along the same lines?

As I previously mentioned, my opinion is that the sports car is 'in the eye of the beholder'. I also think it is 'in time', i.e. one has to take into account the era a given car appeared, and also 'in location', i.e. where it is made and/or sold. By this latter point, I mean that, for example, Britain created small, nimble sports cars that were ideally suited for the narrow, twisting lanes and small towns that originally developed with the horse as the prime source of transportation. America, by contrast, where space, metal, money and fuel were plentiful, produced much bigger cars, which were not required to corner nearly as much as their European counterparts. They were, however, required to travel very long distances – hence the rise of large, under-stressed engines.

The three factors that seem to be in common across the years, however, are that such a car has two seats, with a focus on performance and an essential element of 'fun' – the former being mainly objective and the latter mainly subjective.

In the very early years of motoring, the top-end 'sports' cars may have been powered by aero engines and have been monstrous in dimension and demeanour. Later, sports cars became small and simple, and then bigger, more complicated and required to do much more than just the above triumvirate.

The Corvette was a product of the USA, where space and material were, and still are, in great abundance. As times changed, so did the Corvette, not least in terms of customer requirements. Many a sports car manufacturer has come and gone in the sixty-plus years of Corvette production (so far); the reasons for that are legion, but may include the want of remembering customers and their changing needs. The globalisation effect has also had an impact, in that they need to look beyond their own shores for sales.

Latterly, Corvettes have become more complicated, as have other cars, and are surprisingly good for travelling long distances (in line with competitors) while retaining good performance.

Is anybody in any doubt that we are in an era when the pursuit of power and performance has never been fiercer or more effective? Competition is tough and the market is crowded. No one can argue that any Corvette is without fault, but it has always managed to offer an awful lot of car for relatively little money. In its home country, it has an enormous following of faithful fans and owners, while a sub-culture of clubs, events, merchandise, spares, repairs and performance-enhancing parts has sprung up, employing countless thousands and generating vast sums of money. This is, no doubt, helped considerably by the fact that over 80 per cent of the more than 1.6 million Corvettes made are still on the road.

Away from its homeland, the Corvette is much rarer. In the UK, there are fewer Corvettes registered than Lamborghinis and around a third of the number of Ferraris. A Corvette of some generation and in reasonable condition can often be bought for less than the resultant cost of a full service on one of Maranello's models. Here and on mainland Europe, the Corvette adds exclusivity at a price few would believe.

In each era of Corvette, the car has managed to provide levels of performance and fun for two people that have been at the forefront of what has been available at the time, be it the muscle car era, the fuel-crisis era or today's era of super cars.

In the end, it only matters what YOU think. I get a lot of fun and enjoyment from my 'Vette and, as such, to me it is a sports car, a beautiful one, and I love it. So, I suspect, do the hundreds of thousands of other owners across the globe. Long may they continue to do so.

Appendix 1: Muscle Cars and the Corvette

The muscle-car era was underway as the C2 emerged and in full swing by the time the C3 appeared in 1968. All the American manufacturers were locked in a horsepower battle with each other. Enthusiasts of the genre may have slightly different views on when and who started it, but it is difficult to pin down. We know the 'moonshiners' were tuning their cars in the early 1920s and the police had responded in kind. The latter years of the 1950s saw the new OHV V8s become optional in mainstream cars, giving them performance unseen since the marvellous supercars of the 1920s and '30s, the Duesenbergs, the Cords and the Auburns. Those were the province only of the very wealthy, but the later offerings were for people of much more modest means. We all know that a little old lady from Pasadena had a brand-new, shiny red Super Stock Dodge, which was a barely disguised drag racer with an acid-dipped body and, suddenly it seemed, everyone was in on the act. Big Block engines were available in a whole manner of full-size cars, even if sales were still skewed towards their lesser-equipped brethren, and it was the availability of such power plants that was the starting signal for the horsepower race.

The car that probably is most likely to be credited for really moving it all on was the 1964 Pontiac GTO. John Zachary DeLorean was an enthusiast and senior figure with Pontiac at the time, before much later getting embroiled in the ill-fated car bearing his name that was, briefly, manufactured in Northern Ireland before disappearing under a proverbial cloud. Under his direction, the small-sized (at the time) and mild-mannered Pontiac Tempest sedan received a 389-ci (6.4-litre) engine, a 'four on the floor' transmission, bucket seats (rather than the normal bench seats of most American sedans), sports-style wheels and a name shamelessly lifted from a Ferrari. Ignoring the computer game, the letters GT have often been applied to cars that are really nothing of the sort. Standing for *Gran Turismo* or Grand (or Great) Touring in Italian, the name was originally applied to a car that could comfortably cover trans-Continental distances with ease and not to a car that had more carburettors than other models in the range. Ford Cortina GTs were, for example, fun but would not be one's first choice for a car to cross Europe in. The 'O' stands for '*omologato*' in Italian or 'homologated' in English, i.e. it is a model with enough production examples to qualify for production rather than prototype racing (where all manner of specialist racing cars competed and were likely to be far faster than a road-based car that just happened to be produced in small numbers). The combination of small car and big engine was not entirely new in the States, but had generally been the drag racing specials (e.g. the above-mentioned

Dodge) where the engine was not at all happy on the street, being highly tuned and thus highly temperamental. This engine was relatively mild, but was only hauling a small car, which suddenly became a very fast small car. It sold over 30,000 in its first year and the other manufacturers cottoned on quickly.

Duntov had effectively been predicting this and it seems likely that Chevrolet would not want their flagship car, the Corvette, to be outshone in the performance stakes. Thanks in part to its lighter weight (courtesy of the GRP body), its IRS and high-performance engines, they didn't have to worry. Even before the advent of the Big Blocks, the fuel-injected Small Block C2s of 1963–65 were fast enough to seriously worry the driver of any other domestic car. The arrival of the Big Blocks in both C2 and C3 was enough to keep the Corvette ahead. If the L71 option wasn't enough for you, you could have checked the L88 option on your 1967–69 order form and got yourself an aluminium-blocked Corvette, which, oddly, was rated at 430 hp (perhaps to discourage non-racers). This option would add a premium of over 20 per cent of the base-car price. Why would you spend this amount? Because, although officially offering 430 hp, the L88 had aluminium heads and a 12.5:1 compression ratio, needed 103 research octane fuel and produced around 550 hp. 216 were made between 1967 and 1969, which is pretty exclusive considering that 90,268 Corvettes were produced in the same period. Not as exclusive, though, as the two Zl-1s made only in 1969 at an option cost of no less than 99 per cent of the base coupe cost. This was effectively the L88, but with an aluminium block and steel cylinder liners. These two (of which the whereabouts of only one is known, having spent a good proportion of its life annihilating competition in production-based drag racing) were reputed to produce around the 600-hp mark. No one can accuse the Corvette of not trying in the horsepower race.

In terms of roadholding, it is fairly certain that the likes of a GTO, fun as it was, could not stay ahead of a Corvette when the road started to twist and turn. Also from 1965, Corvettes had at least the option of disc brakes. Back on that twisting road, the Corvette driver might choose to stay behind the GTO or similar because it was only a matter of time until the drum brakes on the heavier car started to fade. The other option, of course, would be to out-brake him into a corner and use the traction, power and roadholding of the 'Vette to pull away before fade set in. To me, this shows all the hallmarks of what a sports car should be, at least at this time, in this place.

The argument as to whether the Corvette is a sports car or a muscle car has raged in the States since both the term 'muscle car' and the Corvette arrived on the scene. Muscle cars are, as we have seen, based traditionally on a smaller sedan from a manufacturer's range, whereas the Corvette is a specific model in its own right with only two seats. It appears to me that the Corvette has the potential to match any of the cars labelled as being of the muscular variety, but throws in better roadholding and braking – the natural province of the sports car – plus very different looks. Perhaps then, it offers the best of both worlds; even if it is more expensive!

Appendix 2: The Corvette in Competition – Some Brief Highlights

Corvettes have been raced for almost as long as they have been in existence. This is true of many sports cars but, while official involvement has waxed and waned over time, Corvette Racing (as it is now known) is in full cry and very successful.

Early Days

Drivers such as John Finch and Dr Dick Thompson (aka, 'The Flying Dentist') raced C1s, the latter winning the Sports Car Club of America (SCCA) championships in 1956, 1957, 1960, 1961 and 1962. It debuted in competition at the 1956 12 Hours of Sebring, with five Corvettes entered. John Fitch and Walter Hansgen finished first in class and ninth overall. 1960 saw the first entries at the Le Mans 24 Hours when Briggs Cunningham entered a team of three Corvettes. Again John Fitch, this time partnered with Bob Grossman, finished eighth overall and first in class. Given they were up against such cars as the Ferrari 250 GT SWB, it was a very good result.

Closer to home, Duntov set an official flying mile record in a modified C1 at Daytona Beach in 1956 at 150.583 mph.

The 1963 Grand Sport

One of the most charismatic cars ever made must be the full race Corvette Grand Sport, which came to the fore at the Nassau Speed Week in 1963. The story of this magnificent monster's brief racing life is wonderful, not least because it was another Corvette chapter unsanctioned by the management. It must have been a coincidence that so many Corvette engineers wanted to take their vacations at the same time that year and that they all wanted to go to the Bahamas! Unsanctioned progress seems to be a hallmark of the Corvette and this was not to be the last time it happened.

The Grand Sport arose out of a scheme envisaged by Duntov to raise the profile of the Corvette, as per the famous 'Duntov Letter', which was written in December 1953 to

Maurice Olley. In this memorandum, he pointed out that young people were getting into 'hot rods' (ordinary cars with aftermarket tuning accessories fitted to make them go faster); Ford were catering for this market by providing performance parts and, logically, once a buyer was involved with Fords, he was likely to always buy Fords. Chevrolet was offering no competition. He was, in fact, pointing out what Ford then and most manufacturers now know – that speed sells, even if only by association. The phrase 'Win on Sunday, Sell on Monday' was coined by a Ford dealer as the impetus for getting his business into racing. Likewise, Duntov wanted a Corvette to take on cars like the AC Cobra and the Ferraris of the day and to win races such as Sebring and Le Mans. However, this required 125 street-legal versions for it to be homologated as a production racer. GM's management had agreed to an industry-led racing ban. This was as a result of the terrible accident at Le Mans in 1955 when Pierre Levegh's Mercedes 300SLR, unable to avoid a collision, crashed, killing him instantly. The car broke into three pieces and flew at racing speeds into the main grandstand, where eighty-two people were killed – although, unofficially, this could have been as many as 130, with many more maimed and injured. It was the worst accident in motor sport history. The US Automobile Manufacturers' Association members agreed to a racing ban between themselves, presumably to head off any legislation that might arise. So orders were issued that there were to be no racing cars, but not before five lightweight prototypes were created. These were secreted away, kept out of sight and mind of management, and quietly developed. For Nassau, a full race all-aluminium engine of 377-ci (6.2-litres) displacement was fitted. The engine is a visual treat with its bank of downdraught Weber carburettors and convoluted inlet piping. It is also extremely powerful

The 1963 Grand Sport race car. This is actually a faithful reproduction, but illustrates the drama of the original marvellously.

While not to the exact specification of the original, the engine has downdraught carburettors that are similar to the original and not seen on other Corvettes.

and probably made in excess of 600 hp. The story deserves to be told in more detail than can be done here, but suffice to say that the Grand Sports comprehensively out-dragged the Cobras, Ferraris *et al* away from the Le Mans start of the Tourist Trophy race in Nassau that year, which is no mean feat, and Dick Thompson went on to win. Similarly at Sebring in 1966 the Corvettes' acceleration again left everything in their wake and they were even able to pass Ford GT40s on the straight, which must have been on pure power alone, given the aerodynamics. And this brings us back to the original point of the C2 aerodynamics issue (see Chapter 3). Despite a rudimentary nose spoiler on the Grand Sport, one of the drivers, the late Dick Guldstrand, is quoted as saying, 'The front wheels would come off the ground at 150 mph'. Apparently, only the very bravest need apply! Overall, the Grand Sport cannot be said to have had a really great career (once the much lighter and smaller Cobra went to 427-ci engines), but, for a brief time, this great missile of a car blazed brightly over the sports car racing world.

The Greenwood Corvettes

Born in Indiana in 1945, John Greenwood grew up among GM products, with his father being a GM executive. He started building faster versions (and is credited with one of the first Big Block conversions with his 1964 Corvette) and then race cars. He entered both the Sebring 12 Hour and Daytona 24 Hour races in 1970, but found more success in the Sports Car Club of America (SCCA) race series, which he won the same year. He is known for the wide-bodied race and road cars that bear his name and show considerable attention to aerodynamics, including lift reduction. Coupled to engines of up to 10 litres, the racing versions were very popular with racegoers in the 1970s for their high speeds, extreme noise and patriotic colour schemes. Perhaps the most famous was the 1976 Le Mans entry named *Spirit of Le Mans '76*, which, by happy coincidence, commemorated the American Bicentenary and carried both the Stars and Stripes and the French flag in a flamboyant paint job. It is believed that the French organisers' offer of a government-sponsored financial incentive for Greenwood to race his incredibly popular cars is unique. Capable of producing somewhere near 1,000 hp, the Kinsler cross-ram fuel-injected engines were tuned down for longevity to around 700 hp. This and the dramatic but effective aerodynamics saw the 'Monster Corvette', as it was dubbed by the British press, regularly exceeding 220 mph on the Mulsanne Straight, which is some going for a sports car (as opposed to the full race cars). The car ran strongly until, unfortunately, in the sixteenth hour, a tyre exploded and put paid to their race.

A Greenwood-bodied Corvette is pictured racing in Europe.

A dramatic shot of a dramatic car. A road-going continuation version of the Greenwood Daytona.

A convertible Greenwood-bodied car.

Corvette Racing

Official full factory support for Corvettes in competition did not occur until the last year of the twentieth century, when the Corvette Racing team made its debut. A partnership between Chevrolet and Pratt & Miller Engineering (which builds the cars and runs the racing programme on behalf of Chevrolet), the teams' intention is to race cars primarily based on the current production model. As such, the cars are still identifiable with their road-going counterparts, despite various necessary changes and addenda. As is often the case, some of the lessons learned or developments made in racing find their way into the road cars. The current C7 Z06 shares the weight-saving aluminium chassis, the aerodynamic principles and many engine features with its C7.R racing counterpart.

It is as true today as it has ever been that racing sells. Owners, prospective owners and fans like to get behind a marque and cheer it on. The link with the amazing achievements of the professional drivers in cars that look similar to their own is evocative. So is success.

I have opined earlier that I think the C5 was a pivotal model for the Corvette. It had to be successful. Even before the car was available to buy, plans for racing it at the highest level were being formulated. Given the financial issues GM had, the not-inconsiderable cost of developing and running a racing team must have been deemed worth the risk. While this view was not always held corporately at this time, racing must have been seen as necessary for brand and image promotion. As a result, the C5-R competed for the first time in the 1999 Rolex 24 at Daytona in the GT category. Between then and 2004, the C5-R scored thirty-one victories in the American Le Mans Series (ALMS) with an outright win in 2001 at the Rolex 24, which gave them ALMS team and manufacturer championships in 2001–04. Great as these races and results are, most enthusiasts regard the Le Mans 24 Hour race as the greatest endurance race in the world and the Corvette C5-R took victory in the GTS category no less than three times – in 2001, 2002 and 2004.

The C6.R took over the mantle in 2005 and proved to be a very worthy successor to the 5 with thirty-nine GT1 wins, and championships each year from 2005 to 2008. The car dominated the class with twelve consecutive wins from 2005 to 2006 and no less than twenty-five consecutive wins from 2007 to 2009. Not content with this, Corvette Racing took the C6.R to GT1 wins at Le Mans in 2006, 2007 and 2008. Revisions to the international rules for sports and GT racing resulted in a C6.R, which was the closest ever to the production version. This version won the GTE Class at Le Mans in 2011, twelve other victories from 2009 to 2013 with championship wins in 2012 and 2013.

When the C7.R took over in 2014, hopes were again high, as were expectations. The car and the team responded magnificently with no less than a class win at the 2015 24 Heures du Mans.

Summarising the results of Corvette Racing between 1999 and 2015, we find eight Le Mans class wins, ten ALMS manufacturer titles, ninety-seven wins out of 168 starts (i.e., nearly 58 per cent win-to-start ratio) and fifty-four 1-2 finishes. Quite impressive and hopefully an indicator for the future!

The car that marked the official return of the Corvette to racing and won its class at Le Mans three times: the C5-R.

The Corvette C5R, making a night-time pit stop during a gruelling endurance race.

Another three-time Le Mans class winner: the C6.R.

The latest version already has a Le Mans class victory to its name – the C7.R.

Corvettes don't just race in the USA. A C6R is pictured at speed in a European race series.

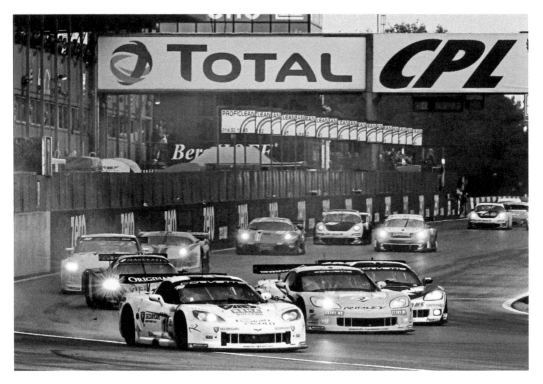

Three C6Rs lead a Maserati MC12 and a field of Ferraris and Porsches in a European endurance race.

The sleek lines of the current generation race car.

Old Corvettes don't die – they just get faster! A C3 competition car.

The C7 logo.